Song Therapeutics & Playlists to Empower Your Life

Nancy Grandits Sabatini, LMHC
Foreword by Jennifer Hamady

TABLE OF CONTENTS

FOREWORD

By Jennifer Hamady:

Music has been one of the greatest passions of my life. When I was a young girl, I sang constantly. And apparently, long before I can remember doing so. Throughout the years, my voice has always been my safe place; a warm and welcoming entity that has connected me to the core of who I am, as well as to my place in the larger scheme of things.

After years of working as a professional singer, I transitioned into a coaching practice, working with others vocalists and performers on the technical and emotional issues that interfere with self-expression. I've written three books on the topic, as well as articles for Psychology Today and others, and eventually returned to graduate school to round out my intuitive work with an academic underpinning in psychology and counseling.

Given my passion for the dance between music and therapy, I was heartened to hear of Nancy Sabatini's work exploring the interplay between these two realms. That Nancy actively shares songs with her clients to help tap into, work through, and release emotional issues and blocks is revelatory. That she has chosen to document and share her approach with those outside of her practice is a gift.

It is clear that Nancy loves her therapeutic work as much as she adores music. And her enthusiasm and passion radiate throughout the book. With inspired musical playlists, helpful journaling prompts, and insightful questions for readers to ponder, <u>Song Therapeutics & Playlists to</u>

<u>Empower Your Life</u>, is a practical guide for anyone asking and seeking to answer the big questions in life.

Which, of course, is all of us. J.

Jennifer Hamady, Founder, Finding Your Voice

ACKNOWLEDGEMENTS

I need to acknowledge and thank my wonderful family and friends who have supported my Song Therapeutics concept and encouraged me to write this book. They were the ones always there throughout the process with great interest, enthusiasm, helpful feedback, and most of all, love. I also want to thank all my colleagues in the therapeutic community. Your willingness to share, ask questions, and make suggestions, and your loyal friendship, have meant so much. Your clinical input has been invaluable. I'm hoping that the content in this book will also help you in your dedicated, committed work with your clients. And of course, I need to give a resounding thank-you to my wonderful clients who continually inspire me in my work. You truly make me a better therapist. Please know how much I appreciate you, your truth and openness, your stories, your struggles, your willingness to embrace change, and your undaunted efforts to improve your life. I am honored by your trust in me and it is really my joy and privilege to work with you, accompanying you during this very personal therapeutic process.

Special thanks goes out to the following individuals for their ongoing advice and consult as well as their support and encouragement over the past year, helping me to make the Song Therapeutics concept and my book a reality: Mike Swift, Larry Van Deusen, and Les Greenbaum. This book is dedicated with love to my lovely mom, Helen Wiles Grandits, who always encouraged me with my therapy career as well as nurtured my love of music since I was a child. She passed away suddenly after a full, wonderful life during the spring of 2020. She is the forever inspiration in my life and remains within my heart, soul, and being, each and every day.

And, especially, a huge acknowledgement and enormous thank-you to all the talented musical artists and composers in the world, who create and share their tremendous gift of music and song and bring this true enrichment into our lives every day!

AUTHOR BIOGRAPHY

I am a New York State licensed mental health therapist (LMHC) with a private practice since 2013, located outside Buffalo, Western New York, specifically in the town of Hamburg. I have been practicing within the field of mental health and counseling in the WNY area for the last 30 years and it has been essentially not only my mission and purpose, but also my overall privilege and passion to do so. My practice focuses primarily on individuals, families, and couples, and since the pandemic started in 2020, I have been providing online teletherapy to my clients. I am always looking for new, creative, and effective methods to connect with them and meet their needs. I am also a consummate music lover, with involvement and appreciation of it being a consistent, fundamental part of my personal life. Combining a love for connecting and helping others through my therapy practice, along with a passion for music, is truly an undertaking of happiness for me as a professional psychotherapist, as well as a person.

THE STORY OF SONG THERAPEUTICS

On an individual basis, I utilize a variety of music and song play-lists to process my own personal thoughts and feelings on a regular basis. It has always made a substantial, positive difference in the quality of my life. In what I considered an enlightening moment working with a strug-gling client several years ago, I realized that music and song lyrics carry truly meaningful messages. It is such a perfect way to connect with people's emotions and reach them effectively, in an enjoyable, comfortable way. I then started to utilize specific songs with mindful lyrics within individual therapy sessions on a regular basis. I chose songs that I felt reflected my client's needs and struggles, songs they could relate to, and that would help them process their thoughts and feelings, helping them to put them into words. When they were verbally unable to identify and express what they felt, the songs made it easier to specify their particular issues and pain. And for necessary follow-through, my clients could remember those songs and use them consistently via personal playlists when needed outside of their sessions. Basically, everything in this process fit in so well with what I was looking for. On a therapeutic basis, I found the results to be quite a remarkable tool to utilize, reach, and assist my clients with their indi-vidual problem areas. As a result, I consistently began offering it to those clients who I deemed appropriate and could benefit from the concept, were interested, and enjoyed using music within their therapy sessions. I subse-quently received substantial ongoing positive feedback from them about the process and playlists and how much they felt this made a marked difference in the quality of their lives.

As time went on, based on evaluating these successful outcomes within my practice, I seriously started thinking about all the benefits of recommending songs and playlists with meaningful lyrical messages with accompanying life skill themes to everyone, even if they were not specifically receiving my counseling therapy. Couldn't everyone basically benefit from this helpful, enlightening information and self-discovery? Hence, as the name implies, the Song Therapeutics concept was born, and this has been the foundation for this book. It has become a major focus for me since then, both professionally and personally. Today, we all need ongoing positive, proactive, comforting messages and life lessons, whether we are involved in a counseling therapy journey or not. Especially now, with the reality of adjusting to major lifestyle changes brought on by the Covid pandemic which has truly enveloped our world. We all continue to need unwavering faith and hope. We need encouragement to keep going, to believe better things are ahead. We need to stay in tune with our emotions. We need to stay strong and never give up. The multiple benefits of the musical experience cannot be denied. Who doesn't want to attempt to understand or make things better in their life and their emotional journey? What have we got to lose? One extremely efficient, yet easy, and enjoyable vehicle available to provide it is undoubtedly music and meaningful song lyrics. I believe you will find the content in this book enlightening and empowering. I think it will really speak to you. Be open-minded, reflect, listen, process, heal, learn... and as we do it, let's all acknowledge the many benefits from this musical ride and definitely enjoy it!!!

*For more detailed information on my private practice, please feel free to go to my therapy webpage, wnyomnicounseling.com

WELCOME MESSAGE FROM NANCY:

The amazing power of music and song, combined with meaningful lyrics and themes, can really help us feel better about our lives. In the listening process, we also discover more about ourselves and what is truly important to us going forward. I invite you to read about this positive journey as you gain new perspectives, explore, and understand our thoughts, feelings, and beliefs, dealing with a variety of struggles and life situations you face every day. This is made possible based on an assortment of great music and songs, from amazing recording artists, with some insightful messages for everyone! Through this book, you have the opportunity to become pro-active and develop the ability to empower yourself, so please, benefit, take charge, learn from these song lyrics, and enjoy the process!

Nancy

INTRODUCTION

How These Songs Will Benefit You

The songs recommended in this book have all spoken to me on an individual basis through my personal playlists. I have also shared their significant messages with my clients, and now, I want to recommend to you, as readers, music listeners, and music fans. These songs are all unique musical gifts to us from a host of talented, brilliant recording artists and musical composers. Overall, they can inform and educate us with our self-awareness, emotional clarity, understanding, and strengthening of relationships, as well as enhance our self-esteem as we navigate the many life struggles we encounter every day. These songs may provide you with a different perspective, a new way of looking at challenges you may face, and provide you ongoing encouragement for making change you may need to consider. The choice is yours, so be open to the process and learn from these songs. And overall, every day, we all want to improve our lives any way we possibly can. This can be accomplished with songs available for listening to empower us, and help us work through any struggles we may encounter going forward. The fact is, listening to a song in itself is certainly not a therapy session. But, without any doubt, the mindful messages provided to listeners within song lyrics, along with the wide range of subsequent psychological benefits, can definitely be pro-active, therapeutic, positive, and healing. It may make a remarkable difference in the process of actually making things better.

In my therapy practice I have consistently seen this happen with my clients as they connect and understand the message, and it's making a positive difference for them. Let my book help you, as individuals who may or may not be involved in therapy, discover the amazing power that song lyrics can provide you as you attempt to understand life situations, questions, or dilemmas you may encounter in your path.

EMPOWERING PLAYLISTS AND LIFE SKILL THEMES

What to Expect with This Book

It should be noted that I do <u>not</u> quote song lyrics in this self help book. But you will have immediate access to my detailed content where, as a psychotherapist, in 18 of the chapters, I will be specifically addressing various life skill themes that may significantly impact the quality of your daily life, such as anxiety, fear, anger, relationship issues, self-esteem, communication, and a host of many important others. Each of these chapters and themes will feature the title and artist of 10 individual songs that I recommend for your playlist that correlate to those varied life skill themes. If you are not familiar with these songs, please take some time to really listen to their meaningful lyrics. I believe these various songs will assist you in understanding how those themes impact your life and how they can in fact, personally empower you with resilience and self-understanding. In my professional practice, I utilize many of those songs within my therapy sessions to connect with my clients in need. I also recommend these songs to clients to use outside of their therapy sessions, to purchase for streaming, listening, and reflecting as part of their personal playlists. Let those songs and their inherent messages become your "go to" helper when in need. With my therapeutic analysis of the life skill themes, I will provide you my input as to why I consider it helpful and needed. I will encourage you to address that theme in your life and thus hopefully make it better. You will also be provided a concise but powerful "take away" thought to remember, which summarizes the general content of the chapter. A series of mindful reflective questions concerning that particular theme will then be provided for you to ask yourself candidly after reading. Here you will have the opportunity to think and journal your thoughts, reactions, and feelings about your life situation as it relates to that specific theme. In addition, at the conclusion of each chapter, you will be given a helpful reading resource about the tremendous depth of music and meaningful song lyrics to add to your library of information and understanding. All in all, providing learning, healing, balance, and relaxation as you discover how music can help you effectively manage your emotional journey.

Yes, we have all heard this phrase before: music is indeed, life! We all need this knowledge and self-discovery and self-awareness, so let this book begin the important process for you. Let the tremendous power of music and song set your mind and heart free to find what you are searching for in life! Let's start with the significant life skill theme of self-esteem.

Chapter 1

Life Skill Theme – *Self-Esteem*

The Song Playlist-

1. "According to You" by Orianthi

2. "Skyscraper" by Demi Lovato

3. "Beautiful" by Christina Aguilera

4. "Firework" by Katy Perry

5. "Stronger" by Kelly Clarkson

6. "Shake It Off" by Taylor Swift

7. "The Champion" by Carrie Underwood

8. "Carry On" by Norah Jones

9. "Born This Way" by Lady Gaga

10. "Dynamite" by BTS

Emotional Needs Assessment -

As a professional therapist, I am always looking for songs that effectively promote the building of self-esteem and empowerment for people of all ages. This theme provides an important lifelong message that is never too early, or too late, to hear and believe. Children need to start off the right way developing this positive mindset and let it grow stronger as they mature. With those of us who care about them, taking the extra time to stop and notice, show interest, comment, praise, and encourage will go a long way in helping them become resilient, independent, capable individuals. Simply put, the subject matter deals with instilling and nurturing an unshakable belief in self, and never letting it go throughout one's life.

Young people are just starting out on their life journey, discovering who they are and ultimately, who they want to be going forward in life. This developmental process can be somewhat tricky as they begin to listen to their own inner voice, they also listen to the voices or opinions of others. If those opinions about them are positive or affirmative, it is wonderful as it builds them up and subsequently strengthens their self-esteem. The problem occurs when those opinions become negative, harsh, or critical, and thus, what does it leave someone with? Feelings of self-doubt, indecision, anxiety, lack of self-confidence, and so much more. Those are all negative messages to absorb. The real danger is, if this harmful feedback continues, in time you come to believe what you hear. In reality, for many young people who may struggle with a developing self-concept, this can often be a troubling message given out in controlling relationships, which they may sadly accept as truth.

No matter how bright and competent people are, if they are constantly bombarded with recurrent negative, critical messages from others, they run the risk of not only believing them but also "becoming" them. This is where developing true empowerment is an absolute necessity, especially in today's complicated and critical world. The fact is… don't let anyone ever tell you you're not good enough, smart enough, capable, interesting, personable, attractive. This is an obvious flashing hazard sign to take caution. If they start to give you those negative messages, it is a signal to seriously take heed and walk away from them as quickly as possible. You know who you are inside and what you are capable of. You control your own mindset. We don't need people in our world to bring us down and make us feel bad about ourselves. Life is difficult enough today without that added negativity. We need people in our life who make us better. Relationships, friends, family, people who regularly encourage us, support us, fortify, and believe in us. You have all the positives stored within you. You just have to discover it, stay aware, relax, and bring it out in your own individual way.

There are a variety of important issues that individuals may struggle with as they go about building their overall self-image. Besides promoting genuine self-love and awareness, there needs to be an ongoing spirit of positivity, never giving up, and being the best you can possibly be. Learning to acknowledge and focus on your many strengths, accept your limitations and/or weaknesses because you are human, but do not dwell on them. Realizing that acknowledging and working on your weaknesses will ultimately make you stronger as a result. It also deals with the possibility of making a decision to consider leaving a dysfunctional romantic relationship that ends up causing you self-doubt, worry, and anxiety. Not settling for those toxic relationships but, instead, searching out those that praise, support, and bring out the best in who you really are. Contentment and satisfaction are the desired results, rather than anxiety and second-guessing due to insecurity. The power of honest, assertive, direct communication and standing up for yourself is essential. I find that for true empowerment to develop before others can love and appreciate you, you have to really love and appreciate yourself. It frankly starts and ends with you. When you think about it, it's such a natural, beautiful thing; so, be grateful and celebrate all you are, and especially are capable of!

Takeaway Thoughts to Remember -

Takeaway positive thoughts empower you, give you strength, make you believe. Here is yours to reflect on. <u>Say it several times a day, every day. Memorize it, write it down, or put it in your phone. In the process, make it a daily routine; rely on it as you make it your own.</u>

Don't ever let anyone, anywhere, anytime take away your belief in yourself! Don't let anyone, anywhere, anytime define who you really are! No one knows and understands you better than yourself; so... believe in your strengths, your positives, your possibilities because your endless potential awaits. Your future is there for you to create and nurture, so do your best to make it happen! And never, ever forget you have got this!

The tremendous power of positive thinking, self-talk and empowering beliefs can seriously help us change the way we think and feel about ourselves over time. Like the well- known term, 'Self-Fulfilling Prophecy", if we truly come to believe and act on the concept, it can become part of who we are, and ultimately, want to be.

With these songs now available on your personal playlist for **building self-esteem**, they will be ready when you need to implement this significant life skill message. Your confidence and ability to deal more effectively with building self-esteem is strengthened as a result. Use it regularly going forward!

Mindfulness & the Music/Questions to Ask Yourself & Self-Reflect –

After listening to these songs, take some time and give these questions some serious thought. Your answers here will reveal a great deal to you about yourself. Use this opportunity for helpful self-reflection on an ongoing basis.

<u>Do you experience periods of self-doubt, and if so, when does this happen?</u>

<u>Do people in your world tend to discourage you and make you feel you are not good enough? If so, describe what happens when that occurs.</u>

Why do you feel you allow that to happen? How long have you felt that way?

Describe your personal self-esteem inventory. What do you think is lacking?

Do you believe your strengths outweigh your weaknesses? Or, vice versa?

Can you acknowledge and make a list of all your strengths and think about them daily?

Do you feel you are generally passive or assertive in your interactions with others?

If you are passive, why do you feel you stand back and let others make decisions for you?

Can you attempt to be more assertive with your communication style? Can you become a more honest, direct, calm, and pleasant communicator?

Do you need to surround yourself more with others who are positive towards you, encouraging and supporting you on an ongoing basis?

Do you feel your parents and family promoted a healthy self-esteem within you growing up? If not, why not?

The Reflective Journaling Process -

Now, take a deep breath, relax, and take the time to really think about your responses to the above mindful questions. What are your reactions, thoughts, and feelings regarding these meaningful questions? Is it difficult for you to provide concrete answers? I encourage you to write down your responses in the space allocated here to save and have access to later. This is your special time set aside just for you. The focus, personal awareness, and self-discovery that result from this therapeutic process will reveal a great deal to you regarding this essential life skill and how it impacts you personally. Your answers will empower you and provide you important feedback about addressing this life skill the very best you can.

Journaling Notes

_____

_____

_____

_____

_____

_____

_____

_____

_____

_____

_____

_____

_____

Recommended Reading about Music & Song-

- *Hindsight: & All the Things I Can't See in Front of Me* by Justin Timberlake, 2018, New York: HarperCollins Publishers.

Chapter 2

Life Skill Theme - *Positive Risk-Taking*

The Song Playlist -

1. "Breakaway" by Kelly Clarkson

2. "Taking Chances" by Celine Dion

3. "Vulnerable" by Selena Gomez

4. "Bella Donna" by Stevie Nicks

5. "Tightrope" by Janelle Monae

6. "It's My Life" by Bon Jovi

7. "No One" by Alicia Keys

8. "Entrepreneur" by Pharrell Williams

9. "I'm Still Standing" by Elton John

10. "Don't Stop Believing" by Journey

Emotional Needs Assessment -

When we think about the term "risk-taking," are we somewhat hesitant with our thoughts or do we focus on the positive aspects involved that may really make us better? What is our general mindset with this very significant topic that can be life changing in so many ways? All of these songs have very meaningful lyrics that make you stop, think, and cover a lot of important ground. Taking action, making changes, believing in yourself, facing fears, indecision, and self-doubt are some essential life skill areas that are touched upon with these lyrics.

Making and then taking the time for necessary self-reflection and self-assessment are encouraged whenever possible. Making sure to do this on an ongoing basic is the perfect way to stay on top of things, and thus keep track of what you need and want as time goes on. This is necessary and helpful because your needs and wants can often evolve over time. Can we see ourself as a person who is thinking, searching, and dreaming. Imagining, envisioning, something different, something that needs to change, something you have been waiting for. Looking at the endless possibilities out there but also wanting that happiness and contentment of mind and heart. Is there optimism and belief in self and especially, is there the hope that something positive will happen? The searching has not always been easy, and people in your life may not have always given encouragement or support in that effort. But, if you are still able to maintain appreciation and persistence and essentially keep the faith in yourself and your potential, that is the foundation. Even confronted with difficulties, fears, insecurities, and self-doubt, determination is needed to keep going with that ultimate goal in mind and the steps needed to get there over time. I find these songs so inspiring because I feel taking positive risks do personally change lives for the better!

The central issue of addressing self-doubt has to become real for you; it truly has to come from within. People in your world can uplift you, influence, compliment, encourage, and give you positive feedback. Of course that will always help empower you, but the belief has to start up within you. You have to own it; it has to be real for you, and you have to put it into action that works for you personally. If you focus on truly cultivating a healthy self-esteem, those periods of questions and self-doubt will occur less frequently. As a result of your efforts, in time you can become stronger, more resilient, more self-sufficient, and subsequently, your ability to take individual action, take positive risks, and make changes will be solidified.

Going about making changes can be scary for people because the end results may not be absolute or readily visible. On the opposite spectrum, considering and embracing change can be quite empowering. This is where the hesitancy of risk-taking comes into the forefront. If you believe in yourself and your abilities, is the subject of taking a risk less frightening to you? Your thoughts may revolve around whether you can realistically handle the outcomes, and basically, be up to the challenge. Again, I am a firm believer in positive risk-taking, and on a personal basis, I have learned to integrate it in my life. If we limit ourselves, if we never take chances in life, if we never take positive risks, we can lose out on many wonderful opportunities that could come our way.

Of course we have to assess the circumstances and particulars of the situation and do what you feel is correct, appropriate, and comfortable for you. That is the foundation of effective decision-making. However, I have seen people burdened with lifelong regrets because they did not take action, make changes, or even consider taking that positive risk. Those regrets can become the nagging, troublesome part that we may really struggle to deal with and understand later on. If you decide to take a positive risk and for some reason, it does not work out to your expectations, what is the worst scenario that can happen? You need to ask yourself that question beforehand and come up with an answer that is suitable for you. If you do make a mistake, do you ever view that as a learning experience that can make you better as a result? Consequences can actually become teachable moments. It should be noted that many people will say that positive risk-taking has not been roadblocks for them. Instead, it has yielded life-changing results that they will always value and be thankful for. Consider all the possibilities that are open to you on your journey, and especially believe in yourself. You have all the power lying within yourself!

Takeaway Thoughts to Remember -

Takeaway positive thoughts empower you, give you strength, make you believe. Here is yours to reflect on. <u>Say it several times a day, every day. Memorize it, write it down, or put it in your phone. In the process, make it a daily routine, rely on it as you make it your own.</u>

Consider the multiple benefits of taking a positive risk in your life. Can it make a meaningful difference that will prove to be well worth it for you? The first step involves conquering any self-doubt and believing in yourself. Facing your fears and indecision may encourage you to finally take action and implement change that may be needed, something that you may never regret. The time is now to consider it!

Remember that the tremendous power of positive thinking, self-talk and empowering beliefs can seriously help us change the way we think and feel about ourselves over time. Like the well known term, "Self-Fulfilling Prophecy", if we truly come to believe and act on this concept, it can become part of who we are, and ultimately want to be.

With these songs now available on your personal playlist for **positive risk-taking**, they will be ready when you need to hear and implement this significant life skill message. Your confidence and ability to deal more effectively with positive risk-taking is strengthened as a result!! Use it regularly going forward!

Mindfulness & the Music/Questions to Ask Yourself & Self-Reflect –

After listening to these songs, take some time and give these questions some serious thought. Your answers here will reveal a great deal to you about yourself. Use this opportunity for helpful self-reflection on an ongoing basis.

How do you personally view the topic of positive risk-taking?

Think of examples from your life where you have taken positive risks. How did they work out for you?

What have you generally learned from the process?

Think of examples from your life where you have taken risks and they did not work out for you? What do you feel happened? Why?

Do you experience periods of self-doubt and indecision? Describe why you think that occurs.

Do you believe you have developed a healthy self-image? If not, why not?

Is change and taking action difficult for you to realistically implement? What do you think holds you back?

As a child growing up, were you encouraged to try new things, problem solve, and begin to make your own decisions? If not, why not?

Do you surround yourself with people who support and encourage your abilities and overall belief in yourself?

The Reflective Journaling Process

Now, take a deep breath, relax, and take the time to really think about your responses to the above mindful questions. What are your reactions, thoughts, and feelings regarding these meaningful questions? Is it difficult for you to provide concrete answers? I encourage you to write down your responses in the space allocated here to save and have access to later. This is your special time set aside just for you. The focus, personal awareness, and self-discovery that result from this therapeutic process will reveal a great deal to you regarding this essential life skill and how it impacts you personally. Your answers will empower you and provide you important feedback about addressing this life skill the very best you can.

Journaling Notes

_____

_____

_____

_____

_____

_____

_____

_____

_____

_____

_____

Recommended Reading about Music & Song

- "The Adaptive Functions of Music Listening" by Michael Hogan, PhD, psychologytoday.com, July 16, 2015

Chapter 3

Life Skill Theme – *Breakups*

The Song Playlist -

1. "Breakeven (Falling to Pieces)" by the Script

2. "Cry Me a River" by Justin Timberlake

3. "Go Your Own Way" by Fleetwood Mac

4. "Nothing Compares 2 U" by Sinead O'Connor

5. "Someone like You" by Adele

6. "Since U Been Gone" by Kelly Clarkson

7. "Somebody That I Used to Know" by Gotye

8. "Fix You" by Coldplay

9. "New Rules" by Dua Lipa

10. "Love Yourself" by Justin Bieber

Emotional Needs Assessment -

There are a wide variety of therapeutic songs out there concerning relationship breakups, which are frequently a complicated emotional process. Overall, the songs on this playlist touch so perfectly on a variety of mood changes and emotions people experience with a breakup. As a listener, you can identify with these common feelings, gain improved awareness, self-discovery, and especially support from the messages presented here. The resounding meaning in each of the songs relates to the assorted ups and downs one can have emotionally when a breakup occurs. We see that parties involved may not take it the same way, and some may experience great difficulty with the aftermath. Is it a cordial, mutual breakup or one that wounds?

The difficulty emerges when one struggles with understanding and accepting a breakup. The shock, the pain, trying to make sense of it, just getting by, and needing strength to keep going. You get a sense of time dragging by, along with descriptions of emotionally falling apart, grief, loss, devastation, sleepless nights, and difficult days. You may soon become aware of desperate love for a partner and feeling lost without them being in your life. This can correlate to the pain that you may feel when that partner has apparently moved on content and happy, having found another person to replace you in their love life. Some may lament that they have lost the best part of who they are, so you get an idea of how deep and consuming the grief and loss can be.

With the theme of relationship breakups, if there is no reconciliation, ultimately there must be a hope for universal acceptance of what we may not be able to change, no matter how much we try or desperately want it to happen. We may not be able to understand or justify the reasons concerning it, but one thing is certain: we have no healthy choice available to us other than accepting the reality of what has happened, as we may never agree or understand the causes or reasons behind a breakup. In this case, accept the fact that both parties may be at different crossroads, one seriously struggling to understand, and the other ready to go on with their life after what has happened. What alternative do we have but to accept? Otherwise, the emotional pain that we create for ourselves may actually become unbearable. So, we have to be proactive and work actively on the acceptance process with the hope and belief that life will be better, that feelings of pain and loss will improve over time, and one will have the full capability to start over and be happy again. We cannot lose that hope. We need that positivity, that unwavering belief in our strength and abilities, and that undaunted determination to go forward. We should never give up, and in that regard, continually keep trying to find the light ahead. It will be waiting for you.

Takeaway Thoughts to Remember

Takeaway positive thoughts empower you, give you strength, make you believe. Here is yours to reflect on. <u>Say it several times a day, every day.</u> <u>Memorize it, write it down, or put it in your phone. In the process, make it</u> <u>a daily routine; rely on it as you make it your own.</u>

With breakups, regardless of who may have initiated it, or if it was mutual, it is important to remember this: with time, you will adjust, and you will accept. You have to get beyond it to be at your best. You have the ability to be strong and resilient within you. The need to continue on with positivity and hope, learning more about yourself in the process going forward. Always believe!

Again, remember that the tremendous power of positive thinking, self-talk and empowering beliefs can seriously help us change the way we think and feel about ourselves over time. Like the well-known term, 'Self-Fulfilling Prophecy", if we truly come to believe and act on the concept, it can become part of who we are, and ultimately, want to be.

With these songs now available on your personal playlist for **breakups**, they will be ready when you need and implement this significant life skill message. Your confidence and ability to deal more effectively with breakups is strengthened as a result! Use it regularly going forward!

Mindfulness & the Music/Questions to Ask Yourself & Self-Reflect

After listening to the songs, take some time and give these questions some serious thought. Your answers here will reveal a great deal to you about yourself. Use this opportunity for helpful self-reflection on an ongoing basis.

Have you experienced a relationship break-up?

Take a few minutes to reflect on your thoughts here. Do you feel the breakup proceeded positively or negatively?

If positive, describe what you feel made it work. What did you feel made the difference?

If negative, describe what you feel made it an unfavorable experience.

Was it a mutual breakup? What were the specific circumstances?

What personal struggles did you face after your breakup? Were you able to resolve them in time? How was that accomplished?

Did you learn any life lessons for the future in adjusting to your past breakups?

In the aftermath of a breakup, how do you approach dealing with a future relationship or a potential breakup now?

The Reflective Journaling Process

Now, take a deep breath, relax, and take the time to really think about your responses to the above mindful questions. What are your reactions, thoughts, and feelings regarding these meaningful questions? Is it difficult for you to provide concrete answers? I encourage you to write down your responses in the space allocated here to save and have access to later. This is your special time set aside just for you. The focus, personal awareness, and self-discovery that result from this therapeutic process will reveal a great deal to you regarding this essential life skill and how it impacts you personally. Your answers will empower you and provide you important feedback about addressing this life skill the very best you can.

Journaling Notes

_____

_____

_____

_____

_____

_____

_____

_____

_____

_____

_____

_____

Recommended Reading about Music & Song

- "Heartbreak and Healing: Why We Love Breakup Songs" by Cristalle Sese, PsyD, goodtherapy.org, June 5, 2014

Chapter 4

Life Skill Theme – *Letting Go*

The Song Playlist -

1. "Change of Heart" by Tom Petty

2. "Better in Time" by Leona Lewis

3. "You Learn" by Alanis Morissette

4. "Let It Go" by James Bay

5. "Starts with Goodbye" by Carrie Underwood

6. "Someone Like You" by Adele

7. "100 Letters" by Halsey

8. "Irreplaceable" by Beyonce

9. "Walk Away" by Ben Harper

10. "What Goes Around Comes Around" by Justin Timberlake

Emotional Needs Assessment

This playlist is one of joy-filled songs and mantras of liberation and embracing change without fear or regret. We need songs of empowerment where one takes a deep breath and exclaims to everyone with faith and enthusiasm that they are now ready to move on! Facing it head-on with a sense of better days, positivity, and inner strength and the belief in oneself. In many cases, it's being ready to move on from a limiting, dysfunctional relationship and leaving it behind, finally, for good.

With our romantic relationships, we start out with eager, open hearts and really want them to succeed. As we strive to make them happen, we are supposed to give them our all. Unfortunately, in love, as in life, there are no firm guarantees that both partners will both put in the same level of effort, love, and commitment. That's the painful part, the frustrating part, the part that we truly can't control or regulate, no matter how much we want it. Here is where the change concept comes into play. Feelings change, situations change, circumstances change and not always for the good. Sometimes we begin to feel used, angry, abused, pushed to the limit, taken for granted, or abandoned. A sense of growing anxiety, weariness, and despair can often overtake us without us even realizing it. Do we just settle and accept or instead, look inward to discover what is really important to us? With time and this growing self-awareness, we may begin to see negative qualities within our partner that we have never been willing, or ready, to see with eyes wide open. Sometimes, a dysfunctional relationship can simply become too trying, too difficult, too draining to continue struggling. We need to realize our whole outlook can benefit when we accept moving on and go forward with that genuine belief in ourselves.

Everyone is strong and capable of change for the better. Yes, it can definitely be scary, unpredictable, time-consuming, energy-sapping, filled with work, and ongoing adjustments. But the bottom line is, if we don't look back and keep going, keep positive, and believe better days are ahead, it doesn't have to be an uphill battle. Most of all, we need to convince ourselves we have the ability and power to do this successfully. Oftentimes, that change is so desperately needed, it can frankly become a lifesaver. So, embrace that fear. The change we come to fear is frequently the best thing that can ever happen to us. It can frankly turn everything around for the better. All of us are entitled to seek and find true happiness, love, calmness, and contentment in our romantic relationships. We deserve it all! We need to be brave and believe we can and will find what we are looking for.

Takeaway Thoughts to Remember -

Takeaway positive thoughts empower you, give you strength, make you believe. Here is yours to reflect on. <u>Say it several times a day, every day. Memorize it, write it down, or put it in your phone. In the process, make it a daily routine; rely on it as you make it your own.</u>

Face your fears head-on, embrace the exciting possibility of positive change, and always believe in yourself. You are strong and capable, and you alone can make it happen successfully and have a happy life.

Again, remember that the tremendous power of positive thinking, self-talk and empowering beliefs can seriously help us change the way we think and feel about ourselves over time. Like the well- known term, 'Self-Fulfilling Prophecy", if we truly come to believe and act on the concept, it can become part of who we are, and ultimately, want to be.

With these songs now available on your personal playlist for ***letting go***, they will be ready when you need and implement this significant life skill message. Your confidence and ability to deal more effectively with letting go is strengthened as a result! Use it regularly going forward!

Mindfulness & the Music/Questions to Ask Yourself & Self-Reflect

After listening to the songs, take some time and give these questions some serious thought. Your answers here will reveal a great deal to you about yourself. Use this opportunity for helpful self-reflection on an ongoing basis.

How do you personally view the concept of change?

Are you presently facing any issue with a dysfunctional relationship in your life? Describe the reasons if and why you choose to stay in it.

Do your thoughts about fear of change ever hold you back?

If so, what are you afraid of?

Can you take some time to become aware and examine the strengths you possess?

Can you begin to identify one to three positive thoughts you could utilize to help you embrace change in your life? Specifically, what do you need to get there?

The Reflective Journaling Process

Now, take a deep breath, relax, and take the time to really think about your responses to the above mindful questions. What are your reactions, thoughts, and feelings regarding these meaningful questions? Is it difficult for you to provide concrete answers? I encourage you to write down your responses in the space allocated here to save and have access to later. This is your special time set aside just for you. The focus, personal awareness, and self-discovery that result from this therapeutic process will reveal a great deal to you regarding this essential life skill and how it impacts you personally. Your answers will empower you and provide you important feedback about addressing this life skill the very best you can.

Journaling Notes

_____

_____

_____

_____

_____

_____

_____

_____

_____

_____

_____

_____

_____

Recommended Reading about Music & Song

- *This Is Your Brain on Music* by Dan Levitin, PhD, 2006, New York: Dutton Penguin Books.

Chapter 5

Life Skill Theme – *Hurt/Emotional Pain*

The Song Playlist -

1. "Everybody Hurts" by Michael Stipe/R.E.M.

2. "Breathin'" by Ariana Grande

3. "Save Myself" by Ed Sheeran

4. "Million Reasons" by Lady Gaga

5. "Love This Pain" by Lady Antebellum

6. "Creep" by Radiohead

7. "Linger" by the Cranberries

8. "Writer in the Dark" by Lorde

9. "Hallelujah" by Leonard Cohen

10. "Back to Black" by Amy Winehouse

Emotional Needs Assessment

I use this playlist frequently working with people dealing with anxiety and depression. All the songs here seem to capture the mood so perfectly. The theme focuses on the fact that we all have our universal struggles and stressors with hurt and emotional pain that we are forced to deal with every day. Especially realizing that we are not alone and the reality that overwhelming hurt and pain may unfortunately come to everyone at some point in their life.

Many can relate to those long difficult days and sleepless nights worrying and not knowing exactly where to turn for help. Wondering if you have the strength to be able to go on and unsure if you will be able to manage anymore of the struggle. Feeling as though everything around you is wrong and confusing, and not sure just how to proceed going forward. Anxiety can certainly overtake us, causing such tremendous self-doubt in our coping abilities and questioning our path to go on. Anxieties realistically need to be embraced head-on. We have to deal with them; we have to process them fully to understand and plan a workable course ahead.

If we don't take the opportunity, time, awareness, and energy to work on our anxieties, they can often continue and have the potential for developing into a full-fledged depression, which can be tricky to overcome. This is where the intervention of a professional counseling therapist can provide tremendous assistance to you. Take the opportunity to seek one out, they will certainly be there for you. No matter how daunting or frightening it may appear, you cannot give up the process. You must hang on with positivity and the ultimate hope and belief that somehow, someway, it will get better. Also allow the help, support, and comfort that friends and family will provide you along the way. They will also be there for you if you let them come in. You will find that beam of light at the end of the tunnel. You will find your way out of the darkness. Always believe.

Takeaway Thoughts to Remember -

Takeaway positive thoughts empower you, give you strength, make you believe. Here is yours to reflect on. <u>Say it several times a day, every day. Memorize it, write it down, or put it in your phone. In the process, make it a daily routine; rely on it as you make it your own.</u>

No matter what you may be struggling with. No matter how difficult or impossible it may seem. Never ever lose hope in yourself and your ability to turn things around for the better. Everyone goes through questions, struggles, and crisis situations sometime in their life. Know that you are not alone, and believe it will get better!!!

Again, remember that the tremendous power of positive thinking, self-talk and empowering beliefs can seriously help us change the way we think and feel about ourselves over time. Like the well- known term, 'Self-Fulfilling Prophecy", if we truly come to believe and act on the concept, it can become part of who we are, and ultimately, want to be.

With these songs now available on your personal playlist for *hurt/ emotional pain*, they will be ready when you need and implement this significant life skill message. Your confidence and ability to deal more effectively with hurt and emotional pain is strengthened as a result! Use it regularly going forward!

Mindfulness & the Music/Questions to Ask Yourself & Self-Reflect

After listening to the songs, take some time and give these questions some serious thought. Your answers here will reveal a great deal to you going forward. Use this opportunity for helpful self-reflection.

<u>How do you generally deal with your personal anxiety?</u>

<u>Do you feel it tends to overwhelm you? If yes, why is that?</u>

<u>Are you currently dealing with any specific anxieties or depression?</u>

What do you do to manage your anxieties or depression more effectively?

How does that help you make things better?

Do you have the tendency to reach out to others when you are feeling anxious or depressed?

If not, why do you keep these feelings to yourself?

Have you ever sought out professional counseling therapy for your anxiety and/or depression?

If you had any advice for anyone struggling with anxiety or depression, what would it be?

The Reflective Journaling Process

Now, take a deep breath, relax, and take the time to really think about your responses to the above mindful questions. What are your reactions, thoughts, and feelings regarding these meaningful questions? Is it difficult for you to provide concrete answers? I encourage you to write down your responses in the space allocated here to save and have access to later. This is your special time set aside just for you. The focus, personal awareness, and self-discovery that result from this therapeutic process will reveal a great deal to you regarding this essential life skill and how it impacts you personally. Your answers will empower you and provide you important feedback about addressing this life skill the very best you can.

Journaling Notes

_____

_____

_____

_____

_____

_____

_____

_____

_____

_____

_____

_____

Recommended Reading about Music & Song

- "Using Music in Times of Anxiety" by Scott Redding, healthblog.uofmhealth.org, May 5, 2020

Chapter 6

Life Skills Theme – *Friendship*

The Song Playlist -

1. "Real Friends" by Camila Cabello

2. "Count on Me" by Bruno Mars

3. "Lean on Me" by Bill Withers

4. "You've Got a Friend" by Carole King

5. "I Turn to You" by Christina Aguilera

6. "My Old Friend" by Tim McGraw

7. "You're My Best Friend" by Queen

8. "We're Going to Be Friends" by The White Stripes

9. "My Best Friend" by Weezer

10. "Friendship" by Chris Stapleton

Emotional Needs Assessment

This playlist is really full of a lot of emotional depth and feeling regarding the topic of true friendship. Most people have an assortment of friends and acquaintances in their life. The question then arises as to how many of those identified can actually be considered real, true friends, basically the loyal kind that are there for you through thick and thin.

Clients routinely express some sadness and frustration relating to an up-and-down struggle finding those special, dependable friends in life, something we can all honestly relate to. A common thought with this theme deals with the feeling of being let down by friends you allow into your life. Having that initial positive outlook but, ultimately over time, being disappointed when the "real" friendship sought after might not actually be there in the end. You feel a sense of growing weary, trying to identify those specific friends and feeling as though realistically, it may never happen. Your level of trust may be impaired as you ask yourself ongoing reflective questions as to why the process is so challenging. You want and need to connect, talk, laugh, understand, and share thoughts and feelings with genuine friends you can count on. Engaging in meaningless or insincere conversations is a part of life but is not actively sought out, as many consider it a waste of time and positive energy. We all can understand why with continued frustration, we may want to be alone and not reach out to others anymore. However, I feel everyone needs and wants to truly believe in the gift of real, true friendship again and should not give up. Simply, it is out there.

With time, self-reflection, and awareness, we all realize the importance and value of establishing a core of real, true friends in our life. The friends who accept you as you are, flaws and all. The friends who are happy when you are happy and don't feel the need to change you if you are not ready. The friends you can count on to always be there to support and encourage you, especially when you are discouraged and weak and can't seem to go that extra step. They will be there, waiting, ready to pick you up when you are struggling, down, or feeling immobilized. People come to a discovery in time that those are the friendships that really matter. Those are the friendships they have to seek out, identify, maintain, promote, and nurture so that these essential ties remain part of their lives. It takes continued work, effort, and commitment that may not always be simple or easy to do. But, overall, it will be so worth it, having these superb friends in your life, hopefully forever. We also need to ask and assess in this process, can we ourselves truly become those "real" friends who are there for others? If not, we may need to look inward, think clearly, self-assess and if needed, make some necessary change. We need to be up to the task and the challenge of giving that wonderful gift of ourselves to others!

Takeaway Thoughts to Remember-

Takeaway positive thoughts empower you, give you strength, make you believe. Here is yours for the week. <u>Say it several times a day, every day.</u> <u>Memorize it, write it down, or put it in your phone. In the process, make it a daily routine; rely on it as you make it your own.</u>

True friendship is a gift to us all, whether given or received; we need to truly value and nurture it. It doesn't come along all the time and once solidly established with love, if taken care of, can last a lifetime! Treasure it and be that quality forever friend who makes a difference in someone's life.

Again, remember that the tremendous power of positive thinking, self-talk and empowering beliefs can seriously help us change the way we think and feel about ourselves over time. Like the well- known term, 'Self-Fulfilling Prophecy", if we truly come to believe and act on the concept, it can become part of who we are, and ultimately, want to be.

With these songs now available on your personal playlist for *friend-ships*, they will be ready when you need and implement this significant life skill message. Your confidence and ability to deal more effectively with friendship is strengthened as a result! Use it regularly going forward!

Mindfulness & the Music/Questions to Ask Yourself & Self-Reflect

After listening to the songs, take some time and give these questions some serious thought. Your answers here will reveal a great deal to you about yourself. Use this opportunity for helpful self-reflection on an ongoing basis.

What does real or true friendship mean to you?

In your life thus far, have you been disappointed with your choice of friends?

Can you say without doubt that you have "real" friends in your life? Identify them.

Can you say in your life thus far that you have friends who have turned out negatively, that is, not been "real" friends to you? Identify them.

On a personal level, what do you find to be the characteristics you specifically look for in a friend?

Why do you feel that is so important to you when you assess friends in your life?

Have you had to ignore and/or remove friends that have not proven to be positive for you going forward? In what way?

Do you consider yourself to be a real friend to others? What do you try to do that makes you a "real" friend?

The Reflective Journaling Process -

Now, take a deep breath, relax, and take the time to really think about your responses to the above mindful questions. What are your reactions, thoughts, and feelings regarding these meaningful questions? Is it difficult for you to provide concrete answers? I encourage you to write down your responses in the space allocated here to save and have access to later. This is your special time set aside just for you. The focus, personal awareness, and self-discovery that result from this therapeutic process will reveal a great deal to you regarding this essential life skill and how it impacts you personally. Your answers will empower you and provide you important feedback about addressing this life skill the very best you can.

Journaling Notes

_____

_____

_____

_____

_____

_____

_____

_____

_____

_____

_____

Recommended Reading about Music & Song -

- "How Music Bonds Us Together" by Jill Suttie, greatergood. berkeley.edu, June 28th, 2016

Chapter 7

Life Skill Theme – *Grief/Loss*

The Song Playlist

1. "I'll See You in My Dreams" by Bruce Springsteen

2. "Let It Be" by the Beatles

3. "Angel" by Sarah McLachlan

4. "Tears in Heaven" by Eric Clapton

5. "There You'll Be" by Faith Hill

6. "Beloved" by Mumford & Sons

7. "If Tomorrow Never Comes" by Garth Brooks

8. "Knockin' On Heaven's Door" by Bob Dylan

9. "Fire and Rain" by James Taylor

10. "Free Bird" by Lynyrd Skynyrd

Emotional Needs Assessment

So many people have requested I feature a song playlist about dealing with one's grief and loss. Such an important theme that will eventually touch everyone in their life at one point or another. A theme of universal need that we all share in this life. On a personal level, for me, I experienced the devastating, life-altering loss of my mother in June of 2020. I had been searching for a ready playlist that meant something meaningful to me concerning my grief and loss. Something that I could identify and relate to, something that would be available and waiting for me when I was struggling and felt sad about missing her presence. There are many lovely, helpful songs out there about the theme of grief and loss. This playlist, in particular, I feel is an excellent one for helping you process these significant thoughts and feelings of grief and loss, and thus move you forward effectively in your life journey.

In this playlist, besides the reality of missing someone who will not be returning in this physical life, it radiates that sense of genuine positivity and especially love and hope for the future. Hearing the message in these song lyrics about life, death, and forever love, the topic of loss appears less fearful and apprehensive to approach. Personally, I walk away after listening to the words with a simple yet significant message. The beauty of it centers on those things I have been searching for and I feel I have found. Those thoughts that give me comfort, peace, and contentment, with accepting what is, and specifically, what I realize I can't change no matter how much I want to. The core centers around the resounding, everlasting love for that person who is gone yet never really leaves you, always there, accessible to you in your thoughts and memory bank when needed, deep within your heart and mind.

This playlist fully acknowledges your grief, but overall, I hear less of a sense of darkness and gloom and more of a comfortable, positive, joyful remembrance coupled with that reality of personal loss. On a personal level I see a sense of optimism, faith, and the joy of experiencing genuine love along with hope-filled thoughts of eventually reuniting with my loved one/s, along with powerful, beautiful memories that will remain with me forever. But regardless of your own personal thoughts and feelings concerning the subject of death, grief, and loss, yes, in my opinion, we can all benefit from that belief that experiencing real love is indeed something beautiful and eternal that can never really leave us.

Takeaway Thoughts to Remember -

Takeaway positive thoughts empower you, give you strength, make you believe. Here is yours for the week. Say it several times a day, every day. Memorize it, write it down, or put it in your phone. In the process, make it a daily routine; rely on it as you make it your own.

When you say you truly loved someone in your life, in essence, when they depart from you, they will always be with you. Touching your life, they leave a significant imprint on you and you on them. Thus, you are forever changed by that interaction. You always learn and hopefully, as a result, take away something positive from them, that helps you grow as a person in meaningful ways. You carry their everlasting spirit within, always part of who you are, whether in your heart or in your mind, through beautiful memories that you will cherish and have forever. Relax, close your eyes, take a quiet moment, think of them, and remember... you will see them as clear as day. Treasure those thoughts, keep them close by, and regularly reflect on the personally uplifting value of them. So, believe and take comfort in this regard as we never actually say goodbye to their forever spirit and meaning in our lives.

Again, remember that the tremendous power of positive thinking, self-talk and empowering beliefs can seriously help us change the way we think and feel about ourselves over time. Like the well- known term, 'Self-Fulfilling Prophecy", if we truly come to believe and act on the concept, it can become part of who we are, and ultimately, want to be.

With these songs now available on your personal playlist for *grief/loss*, they will be ready when you need and implement this significant life skill message. Your confidence and ability to deal more effectively with grief and loss is strengthened as a result! Use it regularly going forward!

Mindfulness & the Music/Questions to Ask Yourself & Self-Reflect

After listening to the songs, take some time and give these questions some serious thought. Your answers here will reveal a great deal to you about yourself. Use this opportunity for helpful self-reflection on an ongoing basis.

How do you personally define the grief and loss process?

What are your personal thoughts and feelings regarding death?

How have you generally dealt with grief and loss that you have experienced in your life?

Has it immobilized you or caused difficulties for you in functioning?

If so, describe your struggles as best as you can.

Do you personally believe the statement "the process of grieving has no time limits"? What are your reactions to this statement?

For those people in your life you have lost through death or loss, how do you generally recover from their loss? What positive actions do you take?

Do you believe in religion or a higher power regarding the topic of death/grief/loss?

What, if anything, do you feel you need to do, going forward, to deal more effectively with grief and loss in your life?

The Reflective Journaling Process –

Now, take a deep breath, relax, and take the time to really think about your responses to the above mindful questions. What are your reactions, thoughts, and feelings regarding these meaningful questions? Is it difficult for you to provide concrete answers? I encourage you to write down your responses in the space allocated here to save and have access to later. This is your special time set aside just for you. The focus, personal awareness, and self-discovery that result from this therapeutic process will reveal a great deal to you regarding this essential life skill and how it impacts you personally. Your answers will empower you and provide you important feedback about addressing this life skill the very best you can.

Journaling Notes

_____

_____

_____

_____

_____

_____

_____

_____

_____

_____

_____

_____

Recommended Reading about Music & Song -

- "Songs of Loss and Healing and the Little Understood Connection between Music, Loss and Grief" by Douglas MacGregor, crosseyedpianist.com, May 11, 2019

Chapter 8

Life Skill Theme – *Anger/Frustration*

The Song Playlist -

1. "Please Don't Leave Me" by Pink

2. "Bury a Friend" by Billie Eilish

3. "Caught Out There" by Kelis

4. "I Don't Care Anymore" by Phil Collins

5. "Angry Young Man" by Billy Joel

6. "Fooling Yourself (The Angry Young Man)" by Styx

7. "You Oughta Know" by Alanis Morissette

8. "Had It With You" by the Rolling Stones

9. "One Step Closer" by Linkin Park

10. "Ballad Of a Thin Man" by Bob Dylan

Emotional Needs Assessment-

The songs featured on this playlist stand out as very honest and primarily focus on feelings of regret, remorse, and the reality that our words and subsequent actions can deeply wound others. With anger and frustration, there is always the possibility of long-standing effects which may not be able to be reversed. In turn, a sense of helplessness can result in addition to the obvious despair, anger, hurt, and disillusionment. The messages sent through many of these songs are very powerful and basically stare you in the face with their intense meaning

For us, as the listeners, this playlist provides us a resounding wake-up call for everyone to think about. And what an outstanding life lesson for us to consider, learn, and always try to remember. Losing your sense of self-control can frankly be easy to do on a spontaneous basis. Do we have a history of recurrent verbally abusive interactions with others? Everyone is dealing with ongoing stressors every day, especially in this trying, challenging time of Covid. Do we take others for granted or wound them with our words? It can be difficult to consistently handle your anger in an appropriate manner. It is quite normal to experience those bouts of anger and frustration, as anger is a common human emotion that everyone experiences. However, it is what we do with our anger, how we understand and process our anger, and specifically, if and how often we engage in negative behaviors that directly result from our anger. Sadly, displacement of anger frequently occurs without our even realizing it. That is where the heartbreaking, wounding words can happen quickly and sometimes intensely. Can pleading and those simple repeated expressions of apologetic words without actual change really make a difference or be meaningful?

Your filter becomes disengaged, and you lash out, many times unfairly, to those you care for and who actually have nothing to do with the true source of your anger. People who are peaceful or passive, people who do not routinely like to engage in disruptive behaviors with you, may be the targets. Why do we feel we may need to be forceful or aggressive to "win"? Why do we feel compelled we even have to "win"? This can begin a hurtful, emotionally damaging pattern that starts up and can become impossible to control or work to eliminate. It calls for a steady, determined plan of looking inward, becoming personally aware, employing candid self-discovery, and being ready to acknowledge those weaknesses you may find. Then, it involves actively working on both your stress reactions and anger management, with the eventual goal of changing it for the better.

Is it possible to salvage your damaged relationship? If you don't employ those measures, and it continues, there may be a time when that person you care for can't tolerate the emotional abuse anymore, may give up on you, and exit your life forever. What better way to take responsibility and show true appreciation and value to those you love. This involves one's personal awareness and taking that plan of action to change and specifically following through with it..

Takeaway Thoughts to Remember -

Takeaway positive thoughts empower you, give you strength, make you believe. Here is yours for the week. <u>Say it several times a day, every day.</u> <u>Memorize it, write it down, or put it in your phone. In the process, make it a daily routine; rely on it as you make it your own.</u>

Hurtful words and actions can wound to the core, with some leading to lifelong regrets. Always take the time to be aware of your patterns concerning anger and self-control. Accept that personal change may be indicated. Take action where required concerning your personal stress and anger management needs.

Again, remember that the tremendous power of positive thinking, self-talk and empowering beliefs can seriously help us change the way we think and feel about ourselves over time. Like the well- known term, 'Self-Fulfilling Prophecy", if we truly come to believe and act on the concept, it can become part of who we are, and ultimately, want to be.

With these songs now available on your personal playlist for *anger/ frustration*, they will be ready when you need and implement this significant life skill message. Your confidence and ability to deal more effectively with anger & frustration is strengthened as a result! Use it regularly going forward!

Mindfulness & the Music/Questions to Ask Yourself & Self-Reflect

After listening to the songs, take some time and give these questions some serious thought. Your answers here will reveal a great deal to you about yourself. Use this opportunity for helpful self-reflection on an ongoing basis.

Have there been situations in your life where you have been wounded by words or actions? If so, what were the circumstances and why?

Have there been situations in your life where you have wounded others with your words or actions? If so, what were the circumstances and why?

Do you harbor regrets over the things you have said? Have any of them stayed with you?

Do you feel you have a good handle on your anger and stress management levels? If not, why do you feel that is? What could you realistically do to improve your self-control?

Do you have the habit of displacing your anger onto others around you? Describe what happens when that occurs. Do you take the time to stop and assess your anger before overreacting?

Do you feel you always need to "win" disagreements with others? If so, why is that so important to you?

Do you have the tendency to take others for granted in your life? If so, who are they and why do you do it?

Do you have difficulty giving apologies and showing genuine remorse to those you have wounded? What could you do better in that regard to show it to others?

How did your parents and family influence your anger threshold while growing up? Did they personally exhibit difficulty with self-control?

The Reflective Journaling Process

Now, take a deep breath, relax, and take the time to really think about your responses to the above mindful questions. What are your reactions, thoughts, and feelings regarding these meaningful questions? Is it difficult for you to provide concrete answers? I encourage you to write down your responses in the space allocated here to save and have access to later. This is your special time set aside just for you. The focus, personal awareness, and self-discovery that result from this therapeutic process will reveal a great deal to you regarding this essential life skill and how it impacts you personally. Your answers will empower you and provide you important feedback about addressing this life skill the very best you can.

Journaling Notes

_____

_____

_____

_____

_____

_____

_____

_____

_____

_____

_____

Recommended Reading about Music & Song

- "Empathetic People Use Social Brain Circuitry to Process Music" by Christopher Bergland, psychologytoday.com, June 18, 2018

Chapter 9

Life Skill Theme – *Facing Your Fears*

The Song Playlist -

1. "Roll Me Away" by Bob Seger & The Silver Bullet Band

2. "Doubt" by Mary J. Blige

3. "We Are Young" by Fun

4. "Tightrope" by Janelle Monae

5. "Hero" by Mariah Carey

6. "I Won't Back Down" by Tom Petty & the Heartbreakers

7. "Stronger" by Kelly Clarkson

8. "Believer" by Imagine Dragons

9. "Unstoppable" by Sia

10. "Fight Song" by Rachel Platten

Emotional Needs Assessment

I wanted to include a playlist of beautiful uplifting songs about life direction, contemplating change, facing your fears, and positive risk-taking. On our life journey, do we end up feeling lost, confused, possibly betrayed, and bottom line, disillusioned with what we have observed from our past? Can we find a significant turning point for a new positive direction?

The common thread here is we all have these perplexing thoughts at different times in our life, at different venues, at different crossroads. We have to pay attention to what these innermost thoughts may be telling us. Basically these messages become extremely important as we go forward even with uncertainty. We all eventually can become empowered with our thinking and will be ready and waiting to make the right decisions we need for our future. As we assess our life, we need to gain the freedom and personal satisfaction that come with the ability to problem solve and ultimately make decisions that feel right. The process continues, but realistically we will probably all face challenges at some point in our life that will be difficult and daunting. Questions that will basically test us, questions that may be impossible to answer. This playlist truly embodies the life skill of facing your fears and positive risk-taking. Believing in yourself and your ability to make sound decisions that are right for you. Being able to analyze situations that arise and problem solve based on what is valuable to you. Looking at life with optimistic, open eyes, resilience, and self-confidence and never giving up. Deep within this core is the ability to keep learning, growing, moving, and searching out what makes sense for you and embracing it with positivity and open arms. If we take away an important lesson from these songs, it would have to be take the necessary time and energy out of your busy day to regularly self-reflect. Always try to contemplate what is going on within ourselves and in our life to ensure it's running smoothly. We owe that to ourselves to have these ongoing essential check-ins to face our fears and keep on top of our emotional well-being.

Takeaway Thoughts to Remember

Takeaway positive thoughts empower you, give you strength, make you believe. Here is yours for the week. <u>Say it several times a day, every day.</u> <u>Memorize it, write it down, or put it in your phone.</u> <u>In the process, make it</u> <u>a daily routine; rely on it as you make it your own.</u>

Staying in regular touch with our thoughts and feelings is essential to maintain optimal emotional and psychological health. These personal check-ins can really make a difference as we navigate life's complicated twists and turns. How we are feeling at the moment, do we need to consider making change, what are the fears we are unsure of, and if needed, how can we make it better? Think about this: If we don't take the time and energy to take care of ourselves and our own mental health, how can we effectively be there for others?

Again, remember that the tremendous power of positive thinking, self-talk and empowering beliefs can seriously help us change the way we think and feel about ourselves over time. Like the well- known term, 'Self-Fulfilling Prophecy", if we truly come to believe and act on the concept, it can become part of who we are, and ultimately, want to be.

With these songs now available on your personal playlist for *facing your fears*, they will be ready when you need and implement this significant life skill message. Your confidence and ability to deal more effectively with facing your fears is strengthened as a result! Use it regularly going forward!

Mindfulness & the Music/Questions to Ask Yourself & Self-Reflect

After listening to the songs, take some time and give these questions some serious thought. Your answers here will reveal a great deal to you about moving forward. Use this opportunity for helpful self-reflection on an ongoing basis.

<u>*Personally, how do you do with the process of self-reflection?*</u>

Do you take time out of your schedule on a regular basis to do this?

Do you experience periods of doubt and confusion in your life?

If so, how do you go about resolving them?

How do you feel you do in the realm of problem-solving?

Are there things you could improve, and if so, what areas need improvement?

How do you feel you do in the realm of decision-making?

Are there things you could improve, and if so, what areas need improvement?

Do you feel you are a strong, resilient person with a good self-concept?

If not, what do you feel you need to do to build those qualities within yourself?

The Reflective Journaling Process

Now, take a deep breath, relax, and take the time to really think about your responses to the above mindful questions. What are your reactions, thoughts, and feelings regarding these meaningful questions? Is it difficult for you to provide concrete answers? I encourage you to write down your responses in the space allocated here to save and have access to later. This is your special time set aside just for you. The focus, personal awareness, and self-discovery that result from this therapeutic process will reveal a great deal to you regarding this essential life skill and how it impacts you personally. Your answers will empower you and provide you important feedback about addressing this life skill the very best you can.

Journaling Notes

_____

_____

_____

_____

_____

_____

_____

_____

_____

_____

_____

_____

Recommended Reading about Music & Song -

- "The Neuroscience of Music, Mindset, and Motivation" by Christopher Bergland/ The Athlete's Way, psychologytoday.com, December 29, 2012

Chapter 10

Life Skill Theme – *Thankfulness*

The Song Playlist -

1. "Room at the Top" by Tom Petty & the Heartbreakers

2. "Thank U Next" by Arianna Grande

3. "Thank You" by Keith Urban

4. "Kind & Generous" by Natalie Merchant

5. "Because You Loved Me" by Celine Dion

6. "I Thank You" by ZZ Top

7. "Your Song" by Elton John

8. 'This' by Darius Rucker

9. "In My Life" by the Beatles

10. "Thank You for Loving Me" by Bon Jovi

Emotional Needs Assessment

I really wanted to feature a song playlist about the theme of gratitude and thankfulness in spite of challenges and negativity we may see around us and the fact that we can still somehow salvage positivity and faith. We all strive for a place where we can gain a true perspective on our life, by way of personal awareness, self-discovery, and being thankful. Somewhere where that sense of hope and belief that no matter what difficulties or pain life throws your way, things will progress onward and, with the right attitude, become better. That clarity of mind, peace, contentment, and especially significant, answers you need should result from this mindful process. I believe after listening to these songs, you will walk away feeling inspired and in an uplifted place, with an improved state of mind.

I think when we step back and take stock of our life, looking inward, closely, assessing, we need to try to refocus with a new empowered attitude, pushing those negatives we encounter into the background. Putting the past behind and getting the important insight that comes as a result of learning from it. Acknowledging and being grateful for the love you have in your life, besides contemplating other things you find valuable. Can you get a sense of clarity of mind, comfort, and peaceful contentment with your journey so far? It may possibly indicate a sense of starting over, going forward embracing change, and a new beginning. It involves facing your fears and not holding back what you feel inside, celebrating, and sharing it. Purely and simply, with this playlist, you are left feeling a sense of celebration, feeling that life is good, and feeling thankful for what you have. We all need that sense of joy, that hope, that belief, to get us through life as best we can. And, we will emerge, even stronger and more resilient than before.

I also approach it in a more global outlook, thinking overall of the big psychological picture. There are so many things we can be truly thankful for. People in our life we care for, that support and encourage us daily. Health of body and mind, our purpose, our faith, family values, our work and accomplishments, our assets, the list can go on and on. It will depend on your individual situation and your personal viewpoint. It may come down to your basic awareness and appreciation for those things that we don't routinely think about and value as much as we should. Those factors are always there, steady, part of our lives, providing us our foundation to build on. Do we take those important, essential things for granted? We are so quick to punish ourselves by focusing on our mistakes, past decisions, and negative reactions we have had. We all struggle with reliving those demons from the past that can be a definite roadblock to staying positive and proactive. The reality is that process takes up so much of our time and good energy, leaves us with less, and thus, we are left feeling worse because of it. That is where discouragement may set in, with your feeling apprehensive, anxious, and depressed as a result. These songs remind us that if we really work on our self-awareness, honesty, positivity, and in particular thankfulness, we can reframe and improve our general outlook. With pandemic restrictions continuing, it is urgent that we develop and maintain that mindset of faith, hope, and belief that eventually our lives will return to a state of normalcy. We really need to practice genuine gratefulness on an everyday basis.

Takeaway Thoughts to Remember

Takeaway positive thoughts empower you, give you strength, make you believe. Here is yours for the week. <u>Say it several times a day, every day. Memorize it, write it down, or put it in your phone. In the process, make it a daily routine; rely on it as you make it your own.</u>

Take the time to really think about the concept of thankfulness, gratitude, and how it applies in your life. Once you reflect and focus on the many positives that you may take for granted, you get a different perspective. That self-discovery and awareness create genuine appreciation, which in turn can change your whole outlook and attitude for the better.

Again, remember that the tremendous power of positive thinking, self-talk and empowering beliefs can seriously help us change the way we think and feel about ourselves over time. Like the well-known term, 'Self-Fulfilling Prophecy", if we truly come to believe and act on the concept, it can become part of who we are, and ultimately, want to be.

With these songs now available on your personal playlist for ***thankfulness***, they will be ready when you need and implement this significant life skill message. Your confidence and ability to deal more effectively with thankfulness is strengthened as a result! Use it regularly going forward!

Mindfulness & the Music/Questions to Ask Yourself & Self-Reflect

After listening to the songs, take some time and give these questions some serious thought. Your answers here will reveal a great deal to you about yourself. Use this opportunity for helpful self-reflection on an ongoing basis.

When you think about your level of personal thankfulness, what immediately comes to mind? Is this something that comes easily for you?

Do you have difficulty identifying things you are thankful for? Why do you feel that is?

Do you generally consider yourself an optimistic or pessimistic person? Do you feel that exhibiting thankfulness improves your mood and mindset?

Do you take the opportunity on a regular basis to reflect or meditate on your sense of personal thankfulness?

Can you easily express appreciation to others through words or actions when needed?

Do you believe you need to become more mindful and grateful for those positives in your life?

What gets in the way of that for you? Will it make a meaningful difference in your life?

The Reflective Journaling Process

Now, take a deep breath, relax, and take the time to really think about your responses to the above mindful questions. What are your reactions, thoughts, and feelings regarding these meaningful questions? Is it difficult for you to provide concrete answers? I encourage you to write down your responses in the space allocated here to save and have access to later. This is your special time set aside just for you. The focus, personal awareness, and self-discovery that result from this therapeutic process will reveal a great deal to you regarding this essential life skill and how it impacts you personally. Your answers will empower you and provide you important feedback about addressing this life skill the very best you can.

Journaling Notes

_____

_____

_____

_____

_____

_____

_____

_____

_____

_____

_____

_____

_____

Recommended Reading about Music & Song

- "When Music Makes You Cry" by R. Douglas Fields Ph.D., psychologytoday.com, September 28, 2017

Chapter 11

Life Skill Theme – *Open Communication*

The Song Playlist -

1. "Say" by John Mayer

2. "Brave" by Sara Bareilles

3. "Talk" by Coldplay

4. "Is There Anybody Out There?" by Pink Floyd

5. "Communication" by the Cardigans

6. "Numb" by U2

7. "On Call" by Kings of Leon

8. "Communication Breakdown" by Led Zeppelin

9. "Hello" by Adele

10. "No Surrender" by Bruce Springsteen

Emotional Needs Analysis -

This playlist is a perfect combination of meaningful lyrics and beautiful instrumentation that really says a lot. The focus is on honest, open communication, getting your message out, and how basic and uncomplicated it is to achieve when we finally decide to go for it. Some label the transparency "I'm just putting it out there," which is truth. By putting your thoughts and feelings into words, it promotes so many emotionally healthy, essential factors that makes a difference in your life. These include having courage, having determination, facing your fears, having faith, having hope, and especially significant, believing in yourself. When I listen to the songs on this playlist, I am also reminded about the potential for regrets. The sadness of it. The reality and finality of things that may never be able to be redone, no matter what. Those "what ifs" that replay in our mind over and over. Some of these regrets don't ease with time. Are we able to accept them and truly move on? The truth is people may struggle with them the rest of their lives. Sometimes we learn by painful personal experiences, which ultimately convince us to change. How many of those regrets could be addressed by taking action with the power of your spoken words. When we really think about it, so simple, so easy. Could those words you say make a positive difference for the rest of your life? Taking a stand, being proactive, saying what is in your mind and heart. So many people will question themselves and doubt their gut instinct. Looking inward, we need to discover what makes us question and distrust our instincts that we need to listen closely and carefully to.

Self-denials and personal defensiveness can sometimes result during our communication efforts. That never helps and will actually hold you back from where you need to go. How many are basically excuses which block you from taking necessary action. We may often hear those familiar phrases recommending open, honest communication, such as "don't beat round the bush" or "don't walk on eggshells." Yes, your communication style, the way you say it, is always going to be very important in the way your message is received by others. Assess your personal communication style, whether it be passive, assertive, or aggressive. Assertive is the ideal goal we should set for ourselves and work towards. The primary keys of assertive communication are open honesty, being direct, and remaining calm and good-natured when you speak. People are going to be more likely to respond positively when you do. Take that deep breath and a minute to focus before the words come out. It takes patience, practice, and determination to have it become comfortable to use on a regular basis. In the end it will be less work and people will respect you because your words really reflect who you are. The results will be well worth it.

Think of it this way: This may be your one and only chance. The opportunity for meaningful communication improves when you simply say what you think. In the effort to promote healthy self-esteem, we also need to be comfortable with this mindset, and it is a process. Being ourselves and saying what we think and feel is definitely empowering. Be strong and face your fears. Fears can unfortunately make decisions for you or stand in the way of what you need to say. The time is now, so consider embracing your communication with an open honest mind.

Takeaway Thought to Remember -

Takeaway positive thoughts empower you, give you strength, make you believe. Here is yours for the week. <u>Say it several times a day, every day. Memorize it, write it down, or put it in your phone. During the week, make it a daily routine, rely on it as you make it your own.</u>

If you don't say it now, you may never have the opportunity again. Don't let it slip away. Remember, it's never too late. Your words make the difference. Bottom line: You know yourself, and the choice is yours alone. It's always going to be up to you. I hope this playlist as well as the analysis presented here help you on your way!

Again, remember that the tremendous power of positive thinking, self-talk and empowering beliefs can seriously help us change the way we think and feel about ourselves over time. Like the well- known term, 'Self-Fulfilling Prophecy", if we truly come to believe and act on the concept, it can become part of who we are, and ultimately, want to be.

With these songs now available on your personal playlist for **open communication**, they will be ready when you need and implement this significant life skill message. Your confidence and ability to deal more effectively with open communication is strengthened as a result! Use it regularly going forward!

Mindfulness & the Music/Questions to Ask Yourself & Self-Reflect -

After listening to the songs, take some time and give these questions some serious thought. Your answers here will reveal a great deal to you going forward. Use this opportunity for helpful self-reflection.

Are you a person who generally says what they need to?

If not, what do you think holds you back?

What do you feel you are afraid of if you're honest?

Do you consider yourself overall a passive, assertive or aggressive communicator?

How do others respond to your communication efforts? Does it get you what you want?

Do you think you need to change your communication style? If so, why?

What have you learned about the importance of simply just saying it?

The Reflective Journaling Process

Now, take a deep breath, relax, and take the time to really think about your responses to the above mindful questions. What are your reactions, thoughts, and feelings regarding these meaningful questions? Is it difficult for you to provide concrete answers? I encourage you to write down your responses in the space allocated here to save and have access to later. This is your special time set aside just for you. The focus, personal awareness, and self-discovery that result from this therapeutic process will reveal a great deal to you regarding this essential life skill and how it impacts you personally. Your answers will empower you and provide you important feedback about addressing this life skill the very best you can.

Journaling Notes

Recommended Reading about Music & Song

- "6 Ways Music Affects Your Emotions" by Shahram Heshmat, PhD, psychologytoday.com, June 17, 2019

Chapter 12

Life Skill Theme – *Addictions*

The Song Playlist -

1. "Sober" by Pink

2. "Chandelier" by Sia

3. "Old Ways" by Demi Lovato

4. "Recover" by Natasha Bedingfield

5. "Hunger" by Florence & the Machine

6. "You Found Me" by the Fray

7. "Demons" by Kenny Chesney

8. "Amazing" by Aerosmith

9. "Salvation" by the Cranberries

10. "One Day at a Time" by Joe Walsh

Emotional Needs Analysis -

The reality in today's complicated world is addictions are all around us. Sadly, no matter what type, they can control us, take away our sense of direction, and leave us desperately struggling. Addictions can slowly start to overtake a person but can also quickly overwhelm. The first step in attempting to effectively conquer addiction is self-discovery and acknowledging you may be experiencing struggles and difficulty. This includes the reality that you may have a problem managing it.

Often, the most demanding part is admitting to yourself that things may have gotten out of control. Honesty is so important. Being able to realistically face your demons and do something constructive about them. Facing the challenge and doing the work necessary to make it happen for you. Your self-awareness and self-reflection can be such an essential tool to jump-start the whole process. We all have a storage of deep inner strength within ourselves. Sometimes it can get buried over time and can be painstaking to find. The reality is that genuine resilient spirit is there, ready and waiting to be called upon when needed, especially useful when addictions may immobilize us.

As a therapist, I imagine any person who appears to be at an ultimate crossroads, in terms of assessing their mental struggle with alcohol or drugs. It looks like after a long time, they are finally confident and ready to make a significant change in their life when it comes to alcohol or drug usage. They are trying to break free of the same old habits and negative patterns that have proved detrimental, feeling comfort and safety there. They may be experiencing high and low feelings, mental and physical exhaustion, drastic mood swings, feeling so very good but then quickly feeling so very bad. They may not be able to exhibit strength to resist the temptations that would continually lure them in. I can feel a sense of pain, weariness, self-doubt and frequent loneliness that would subsequently result after the routine of addictive behavior. I see a desperate attempt for them to become whole again, healthy again mentally and also physically. The person they were before, that person in sobriety or without addictions, and the realization that they can feel good again without the need for or dependence on alcohol or drugs. Building self-esteem, searching to find and value that person again. And the end result, isn't that so worth it? That person who can be their authentic self and doesn't require alcohol or drugs to be their best.

Overcoming personal addictions, whatever they may be, whoever faces them in life, requires a positive mindset, undaunted determination, and bottom line, consistent hard work. No matter what, always believe in yourself with the knowledge that it can be accomplished by only you; you certainly have the power within, and it can indeed set you free!

Takeaway Thought for the Week Ahead -

Takeaway positive thoughts empower you, give you strength, make you believe. Here is yours for the week. <u>Say it several times a day, every day. Memorize it, write it down, or put it in your phone. During the week, make it a daily routine; rely on it as you make it your own.</u>

You have the power existing within you, the power to change your life for the better. The power to turn things around in your life. You have to want it with all you have inside and give it your full effort of heart and mind. It is not easy and takes ongoing work and determination. But it can be accomplished once we set our mind to do it and is so worth it. Face your fears and believe in your inner strength and resilience. Nothing is beyond your scope of accomplishment. You control your life choices; make them the healthiest, both physically and emotionally!

Again, remember that the tremendous power of positive thinking, self-talk and empowering beliefs can seriously help us change the way we think and feel about ourselves over time. Like the well-known term, 'Self-Fulfilling Prophecy", if we truly come to believe and act on the concept, it can become part of who we are, and ultimately, want to be.

With these songs now available on your personal playlist for **addictions**, they will be ready when you need and implement this significant life skill message. Your confidence and ability to deal more effectively with addictions is strengthened as a result! Use it regularly going forward!

Mindfulness & the Music/Questions to Ask Yourself & Self-Reflect

After listening to the songs, take some time and give these questions some serious thought. Your answers here will reveal a great deal to you going forward. Use this opportunity for helpful self-reflection.

What is your personal relationship with alcohol or drug usage? Do you consider yourself a social drinker or something more involved addiction wise?

Has it presented a "functioning" problem for you in your life? If so, please explain.

Can you realistically and effectively control your use of alcohol or drugs?

Do you feel your overall personality changes when you engage in addictions? In what way? Positive? Negative?

How often per week do you engage in alcohol or drug consumption?

Do you come from a family background that generally valued alcohol or drug usage?

Do the people you surround yourself with regularly use alcohol or drugs?

Do you feel you basically have good self-esteem? Does it need strengthening?

Is making change in your life difficult for you? Why do you feel that is?

Going forward, is there anything you personally feel the need to do concerning the use of alcohol or drugs?

The Reflective Journaling Process -

Now, take a deep breath, relax, and take the time to really think about your responses to the above mindful questions. What are your reactions, thoughts, and feelings regarding these meaningful questions? Is it difficult for you to provide concrete answers? I encourage you to write down your responses in the space allocated here to save and have access to later. This is your special time set aside just for you. The focus, personal awareness, and self-discovery that result from this therapeutic process will reveal a great deal to you regarding this essential life skill and how it impacts you personally. Your answers will empower you and provide you important feedback about addressing this life skill the very best you can.

Journaling Notes

Recommended Reading About Music & Song

- "The Power of Music: How It Can Benefit Health" by Honor Whiteman, medicalnewstoday.com, November 19, 2015

Chapter 13

Life Skill Theme – *Forgiveness*

The Song Playlist -

1. "The Heart of the Matter" by Don Henley

2. "Forgive Myself" by Sam Smith

3. "You're Only Human" by Billy Joel

4. "Please Forgive Me" by Bryan Adams

5. "Harder to Forgive" by Brandi Carlile

6. "Blank Page" by Christina Aguilera

7. "Back to December" by Taylor Swift

8. "A Song for You" by Amy Winehouse

9. "Time Is a Healer" by Eva Cassidy

10. "Low Man's Lyric" by Metallica

Emotional Needs Analysis

This playlist focuses on the universal theme of forgiveness with song lyrics so full of emotional depth and tenderness, which involves eventually coming to forgive others. Learning to truly forgive can in fact be a challenging process indeed and not often easily understood. Besides a giving, open heart and perspective, it requires will and determination as you come to really grasp the true meaning and implications that involve forgiveness.

At some point in your life, you have probably been hurt by someone. The level and intensity can vary with each specific situation, but one thing is true, when people hurt you to the core, for whatever reason, it can suddenly change your whole perspective of how you view them. Some may say it's simply a matter of losing trust and respect, but more so, your general attitude towards them in whole shifts dramatically. So we ask, can the hurtful, wounding actions of others help you to see them clearer, for who they really are? Yes, this most definitely can occur. In fact, this can be a helpful personal discovery which can open your eyes and be a powerful reality check for you going forward. However, in a more proactive way, we may need to look at forgiveness from another vantage point, from a different, more open-minded lens. View it as a form of individual awareness and beneficial enlightenment, which should actually be welcomed and appreciated in the long run.

It is important you come to realize that you need to forgive, especially for you. This is where the act of forgiving others becomes visible and makes sense to you as you try to remain at your best in terms of positivity. Forgiveness is definitely an act of kindness, compassion, and giving that we decide to grant others. But, when we begin to think more deeply about it, we need to let it go, primarily for us. In life, people are often reluctant to forgive because they may harbor pent-up anger or resentment. Those feelings can also become intense, very difficult to extinguish and are quite emotionally unhealthy for one to hold onto. We need to change our entire view of the forgiveness process and also begin to see it as a gift you give yourself. The potential benefits of this mindset for our emotional health and well-being are obvious. Who doesn't want to cleanse themselves from negativity and painful thoughts and memories? What is the benefit for you in hanging onto these negative feelings and going forward carrying them? Life can be difficult enough without adding to the mix. Thus, we essentially need to unburden this baggage ourselves, simply through the process of forgiving.

In addition, it is always helpful if we take some time to self-reflect afterwards about the situation and circumstances, as well as the person who has hurt you. This is not making excuses for their behavior but instead taking in consideration what may be going on with them internally, what struggles they may actually be going through. We are all human; we are all experienced and capable of making mistakes, bad judgement calls, and hurtful actions towards others. Decisions are made that we regret and are remorseful for afterwards. But we do know that life has to continue for the best in spite of hurtful people, disappointments, hardships, or losses we endure in life. And especially, we learn and subsequently take away important lessons from these experiences we undergo. Is forgiveness realistically possible for you to give presently, or consider for the future? Have you been successful truly forgiving people in your past? These questions and answers are very personal and have to be assessed individually. However, what you discover may assist you in determining your ultimate choice here.

Part of true forgiveness also involves acceptance. The two go hand in hand, as you cannot realistically have one without the other. To forgive is to accept as well. Forgiveness and acceptance together can create a sense of peace and contentment within yourself. Forgiveness does not need to be an end product of anything negative that resembles revenge, getting even, or settling the score, but the heart saying it's time to finally let it go. Forgiveness may involve accepting things you may not be happy with but you basically discover they are what they are, and you may never be able to change them. Whatever happened which warrants you providing genuine forgiveness to someone may end up being well worth it for you, as well as for them. Compare it to when you take a deep breath, close your eyes, and slowly exhale. You have the opportunity to rid yourself of the negativity that can never do you good. Forgiveness can provide you that needed breath of fresh air, a new outlook, a clean slate with a new perspective to start over with a renewed and hopeful attitude for the future. It is well within your reach.

Takeaway Thought for the Week Ahead -

Takeaway positive thoughts empower you, give you strength, make you believe. Here is yours for the week. <u>Say it several times a day, every day. Memorize it, write it down, or put it in your phone. During the week, make it a daily routine; rely on it as you make it your own.</u>

Forgiveness should be considered a meaningful gift you give others, but more importantly, it is truly a gift you give yourself. To let go of any lingering negativity you may harbor in the effort to focus on rebuilding and self-resiliency. With forgiveness comes acceptance of what has happened, no matter how hurtful, learning what you need to from the experience, and the inner peace/contentment that results as you go forward with your positive journey.

Again, remember that the tremendous power of positive thinking, self-talk and empowering beliefs can seriously help us change the way we think and feel about ourselves over time. Like the well- known term, 'Self-Fulfilling Prophecy', if we truly come to believe and act on the concept, it can become part of who we are, and ultimately, want to be.

With these songs now available on your personal playlist for ***forgiveness,*** they will be ready when you need and implement this significant life skill message. Your confidence and ability to deal more effectively with forgiveness is strengthened as a result! Use it regularly going forward!

Mindfulness & the Music/Questions to Ask Yourself & Self-Reflect -

After listening to the songs, take some time and give these questions some serious thought. Your answers here will reveal a great deal to you going forward. Use this opportunity for helpful self-reflection.

How do you personally feel about the process of forgiveness? Do you view it honestly in a positive or negative way? Why?

Is forgiving others generally easy for you? Why is that?

Did you grow up in a family environment that encouraged and promoted the act of forgiveness?

If forgiveness is not easy for you, why do you think that is?

Are there specific situations and/or circumstances where you feel you absolutely cannot forgive?

Have you received forgiveness from someone? If so, describe how that makes you feel.

If you have not received forgiveness, why do you feel that happened?

What do you feel you need to do concerning your ability to forgive? Do you need to change your viewpoint going forward?

The Reflective Journaling Process -

Now, take a deep breath, relax, and take the time to really think about your responses to the above mindful questions. What are your reactions, thoughts, and feelings regarding these meaningful questions? Is it difficult for you to provide concrete answers? I encourage you to write down your responses in the space allocated here to save and have access to later. This is your special time set aside just for you. The focus, personal awareness, and self-discovery that result from this therapeutic process will reveal a great deal to you regarding this essential life skill and how it impacts you personally. Your answers will empower you and provide you important feedback about addressing this life skill the very best you can.

Journaling Notes

_____

_____

_____

_____

_____

_____

_____

_____

_____

_____

_____

_____

Recommended Reading about Music & Song -

- "Music's Power Explained" by Ralph Ryback, MD, psychologyto-day.com, January 19, 2016

Chapter 14

Life Skill Theme – *Hope/Faith/Joy*

The Song Playlist -

1. "The Promised Land" by Bruce Springsteen

2. "You Found Me" by the Fray

3. "Arms Wide Open" by Creed

4. "Bridge over Troubled Water" by Simon & Garfunkel

5. "One Love" by Bob Marley

6. "From a Distance" by Bette Midler

7. "Imagine" by John Lennon

8. "Right Now" by Van Halen

9. "Shiny Happy People" by R.E.M.

10. "Brighter than the Sun" by Colbie Caillat

Emotional Needs Analysis -

Such a meaningful playlist, which I feel has a significant message for all of us going forward positively in life. Faith, hope, and joy—three essentials that are highly sought after in this life journey.

On a personal basis, what does this theme mean to you? For myself, I immediately think of something positive, something aspirational, something that reflects maintaining a sense and belief in faith and hope. Faith and hope are essentially a foundation of life. When we begin to lose faith, when we begin to lose hope, that is where the true struggle begins. We have to find a way, some way, to believe and hang on to our faith and hope because so much is built upon that foundation.

Especially now, with the Covid-19 pandemic part of our world, our faith and hope for better days, for normalcy in our lives, for our health and well-being is being tested like we have never, ever experienced in our lifetime. Essentially, we are living it each and every day. It becomes extremely difficult to keep ongoing positivity and that faith and hope alive in the face of so much doubt and fear that is inherent in our new normal. So much hardship and struggle, so much sadness and loss of life we have witnessed all around us, and it seems never-ending. Doubt and uncertainty have become part of life with so many emotional, medical, financial, and economic changes creating instability in today's world.. Can we realistically maintain happiness and optimism, when it can be difficult to keep our faith, when it can be difficult to maintain hope?

I find the lyrical messages in this song playlist to be really powerful, and they reflect what can be truly inspirational in our lives right now. I find optimism and a belief in our enduring human spirit, the core of the songs here. On a personal level, when I listen to them, my sense of faith and hope becomes refreshed and renewed.

I imagine the life of a man who has begun searching for something in life to hold onto. A person who lives his life as one should, works hard, is decent towards others, and basically lives what he considers a "good" life.

But yet, he notices something important, something significant is lacking for him. As he reflects on his life, he is desperately looking for something to believe in. There's so much more to life, isn't there? Meaning, purpose, clarity, and especially answers. He is looking for a way to take control of his destiny. I can definitely feel his sense of pain, weariness, and frustration with his past life experiences, as well as apprehensions about what struggles lie ahead. But as he addresses these issues, his disillusionment and fears seem to eventually lead him to a place of peace and contentment about the journey he will need to take. He comes to a point of strength and he is finally ready. Ultimately, through an undaunted positive spirit, and his belief in himself, his faith and hope come through. I am convinced he will, without any doubt, find what he is searching for.

This is truly a playlist of empowerment. Pure and simple, it's all there. We all face moments when we question the path of our life and we continually look for the answers that make sense. Sometimes those answers are difficult or impossible to find. Do we then give up on the process of maintaining our faith and hope? In today's world, our faith may be challenged every day. There is negativity, pain, disturbing things we witness directly, hear, or read about. We experience heartbreak, losses, betrayals, and disappointments that we must accept in life. Things that contribute to anxiety, depression, uncertainty, and fear, all which can immobilize us. The reality is, we can easily become overwhelmed and apathetic and display anger and frustration because we may feel helpless. We are often unsure as to what to do next.

We need to know that we have the inner resources needed to channel those feelings into something positive. In spite of roadblocks, we have to remain strong, focused, and determined to keep going forward with a resilient attitude. Whatever you're struggling with, your attitude and approach makes all the difference. Will it be a positive or negative one? There are no benefits to having a negative outlook, whatever the situation. It will never help you personally; it will never make things better. It just brings you down. Again, facing our fears is not always easy; we have to be willing and ready to tackle some hard work to get through it successfully. The efforts we put into the battle can yield us such remarkable benefits if we don't give up. Oftentimes the end results of that spirit and perseverance can be so worthwhile and life changing. How many times have we heard the expression "good things are worth waiting and fighting for"?

I believe in the core of our basic American spirit, which I feel is based on faith and hope. In spite of the immeasurable loss of human life and heartache, we will get through this pandemic crisis. We have to; it's what we do. I feel we will become stronger, wiser, more connected, and more empathic people as a result. From coast to coast, we are the American people, known throughout the world for our merciful hearts and indomitable spirit that never gives up!

Takeaway Thought for the Week Ahead

Takeaway positive thoughts empower you, give you strength, make you believe. Here is yours for the week. Say it several times a day, every day. Memorize it, write it down, or put it in your phone. During the week, make it a daily routine; rely on it as you make it your own.

Never lose hope. Hope essentially provides you the faith needed to keep going, even when things seem impossible. Faith and hope give you a purpose to believe in and ultimately work towards achieving. Trust the process; you will find a way.

Again, remember that the tremendous power of positive thinking, self-talk and empowering beliefs can seriously help us change the way we think and feel about ourselves over time. Like the well- known term, 'Self-Fulfilling Prophecy", if we truly come to believe and act on the concept, it can become part of who we are, and ultimately, want to be.

With these songs now available on your personal playlist for *hope, faith, joy*, they will be ready when you need and implement this significant life skill message. Your confidence and ability to deal more effectively with building hope, faith and joy, are strengthened as a result! Use it regularly going forward!

Mindfulness & the Music/Questions to Ask Yourself & Self-Reflect -

After listening to the songs, take some time and give these questions some serious thought. Your answers here will reveal a great deal to you going forward. Use this opportunity for helpful self-reflection.

Describe your personal "Promised Land"? Why is that important to you?

When you think of the term "faith," what does it mean to you?

What do you hope for at this point in your life?

Are there times when you doubt yourself? When does that happen and why?

Do your fear and apprehensions hold you back? Why do you feel that is?

What do you think you need to do to improve your individual sense of faith and hope?

The Reflective Journaling Process

Now, take a deep breath, relax, and take the time to really think about your responses to the above mindful questions. What are your reactions, thoughts, and feelings regarding these meaningful questions? Is it difficult for you to provide concrete answers? I encourage you to write down your responses in the space allocated here to save and have access to later. This is your special time set aside just for you. The focus, personal awareness, and self-discovery that result from this therapeutic process will reveal a great deal to you regarding this essential life skill and how it impacts you personally. Your answers will empower you and provide you important feedback about addressing this life skill the very best you can.

Journaling Notes

_____

_____

_____

_____

_____

_____

_____

_____

_____

_____

_____

Recommended Reading about Music & Song

- "Why Are We Moved by Music?" by Shahram Heshmat, PhD, psychologytoday.com, July 24, 2018

Chapter 15

Life Skill Theme – *Anxiety/Depression*

The Song Playlist -

1. "This Is It" by Kenny Loggins

2. "Skyscraper" by Demi Lovato

3. "Demons" by Imagine Dragons

4. "Keep Breathing" by Ingrid Michaelson

5. "Better Place" by Rachel Platten

6. "Human" by Christina Perri

7. "Give Me Love" by Ed Sheeran

8. "Fix You" by Coldplay

9. "True Love" by Radiohead

10. "End of the Day" by Beck

Emotional Needs Analysis

Whether dealing with unstable relationships or your own individual anxieties, this playlist is a definite go-to for empowerment! It can help make you more resilient, determined, and purposeful going forward, whatever challenges life may be throwing your way. After you listen to the songs, on a personal level, hopefully you will feel better, more positive, and ready, almost enthusiastic, to face what worries are put in front of you.

This playlist embodies the will to survive, to always believe in your abilities to fight and never give up, no matter what the struggle may involve. That instinct is an integral part of our heart and soul, yet sometimes it becomes weakened or lost with the demands of our very hectic and complicated lives. Sometimes self-doubts will plague us and cause us apprehension. Anxieties we face and depression that often results can make this essential process somewhat tricky. We become overwhelmed and unsure, and our inner strength is questioned. But when that occurs, we have to convince ourselves and know what we need to say to make it happen. So simple, right? This is our opportunity, our moment, our chance to turn it around, to try to make it what we want it to be. There should be no hesitancy or turning back once we feel willing and ready to do it. Now or never. Are we up to the challenge? Yes, we all possess that ability within us; we just have to be aware and choose it, believe in ourselves, and try. This is our personal miracle we hold right within our hands.

As professional therapists, we all attempt to encourage and help instill this mantra within our clients coming to us with their anxieties and depression. Our clients vent and share their innermost thoughts and feelings, and we respond by providing support, information, and honest therapeutic feedback for their benefit. But it is important to remember that the true work, the process, the change has to realistically come from within our clients themselves. In other words, they make it actually happen, we don't, no matter how much we influence their frame of mind. So, the power always lies within you. As you face your fears, don't run away or hide but, decide to bravely go there. The time is now to be bold. Avoiding the process or blocking it out never helps in the long run. It just prolongs your emotional struggle. The best advice for dealing with anxieties and subsequent depression is to do the necessary work to find out what is going on and develop a plan of action that is doable for you. Therapists will definitely help you do that, but it is ultimately up to you to make the actions realistically happen. Cultivating the right mindset can certainly be the start to making it happen!

Takeaway Thought for the Week Ahead

Takeaway positive thoughts empower you, give you strength, make you believe. Here is yours for the week. <u>Say it several times a day, every day. Memorize it, write it down, or put it in your phone. During the week, make it a daily routine; rely on it as you make it your own.</u>

You alone have the power and ability to change your life. You will be the one to make it happen, so be ready and willing to go there when you have to. Look inward, believe in yourself, and trust your instincts during this self-learning process. You will determine what is doable and realistic for you. Go there when you need to. This is the core!

Again, remember that the tremendous power of positive thinking, self-talk and empowering beliefs can seriously help us change the way we think and feel about ourselves over time. Like the well- known term, 'Self-Fulfilling Prophecy", if we truly come to believe and act on the concept, it can become part of who we are, and ultimately, want to be.

With these songs now available on your personal playlist for *anxiety/ depression,* they will be ready when you need and implement this significant life skill message. Your confidence and ability to deal more effectively with your anxieties and depression is strengthened as a result! Use it regularly going forward!

Mindfulness & the Music/Questions to Ask Yourself & Self-Reflect -

After listening to the songs, take some time and give these questions some serious thought. Your answers here will reveal a great deal to you going forward. Use this opportunity for helpful self-reflection.

<u>*Do you have recurrent issues with bouts of anxiety and depression?*</u>

Do you believe in your ability to "figure things out"?

Do you struggle with feelings of self-doubt? If so, why?

What is your problem-solving ability like? Is it rushed, or slow and thoughtful?

What is your decision-making ability like? Are you hesitant or dependent on other's input?

Are you currently receiving individual counseling therapy? Does it help you in this process?

Did your parents or family encourage you to believe in your ability to sort things out?

What are your fears about engaging in this process? Can you let them go?

The Reflective Journaling Process

Now, take a deep breath, relax, and take the time to really think about your responses to the above mindful questions. What are your reactions, thoughts, and feelings regarding these meaningful questions? Is it difficult for you to provide concrete answers? I encourage you to write down your responses in the space allocated here to save and have access to later. This is your special time set aside just for you. The focus, personal awareness, and self-discovery that results from this therapeutic process will reveal a great deal to you regarding this essential life skill and how it impacts you personally. Your answers will empower you and provide you important feedback about addressing this life skill the very best you can.

Journaling Notes

_____

_____

_____

_____

_____

_____

_____

_____

_____

_____

_____

_____

Recommended Reading about Music & Song

- "How Music Is a Catalyst for Renewal, Recovery, and Rebirth" by Christopher Bergland, psychologytoday.com, April 24, 2019

Chapter 16

Life Skill Theme – *Determination/Persistence*

The Song Playlist -

1. "Tiny Victories" by Christina Perri

2. "Just Fine" by Mary J. Blige

3. "Feelin' Good" by Nina Simone

4. "Don't Give Up" by Peter Gabriel

5. "Hold On" by Wilson Phillips

6. "I Won't Back Down" by Tom Petty

7. "Keep Holding On" by Avril Lavigne

8. "I'm Still Standing" by Elton John

9. "You're Only Human" by Billy Joel

10. "Nothing Else Matters" by Metallica

Emotional Needs Analysis

This is another great playlist to enhance one's self-esteem and empowerment. I consider it an excellent mantra to have on hand when those periods of doubt unfortunately set in and we need a quick dose of positive reinforcement. Facing so many of those emotional struggles we may wrestle with believing in ourselves. Looking in the mirror and not liking what we see in the reflection. Times when we simply want to become invisible and hide ourselves away from everyone and everything. Having a sense of feeling broken and not knowing quite how to put ourselves back together again. Days when we just give up on ourselves and forfeit even trying to make it better. When self-confidence is literally hanging on by a string and we're anxious and unsure what to do next.

If we're aware and truly honest with ourselves, I think we can all identify with these feelings of vulnerability and have times in our life when we have faced these dilemmas head-on. If we go to the heart of the matter, we see the world through beautiful lyrics, which provide hope and a sense of light at the end of the tunnel. We can refer to these issues as battles for self-worth. If we achieve success when we face these issues directly, we can do the needed work to overcome the obstacles. The successes are so welcome and so needed as they help promote self-esteem and empower significantly. This essential process is fluid and continual; it is never stationary. We are human, we all have our good days and we have our bad days.

But there is an important message here that we should all remember. When we have our bad days and times of struggle, we need to deal with them as soon as possible, evaluate them, plan, employ some type of change, and then work hard to make some improvement for us. Those are truly the successes that are meaningful, that count, and make us believe in ourselves. Never giving up, never giving in, but each and every day, trying with very best of our ability and trusting in our instincts, our mind, and our soul. Again, the power is always within us, waiting; we just have to stay the course, believe, and thus make it happen.

Takeaway Thought for the Week Ahead

Takeaway positive thoughts empower you, give you strength, make you believe. Here is yours for the week. <u>Say it several times a day, every day.</u> <u>Memorize it, write it down, or put it in your phone. During the week, make</u> <u>it a daily routine; rely on it as you make it your own.</u>

When fears, apprehensions, and doubts overwhelm you, you need to immediately stop the negative thinking. Instead, take a deep, long breath along with some needed time to fully reassess the situation that lies before you. You are strong, capable, and fully able to figure out what you need to. This power comes from deep within; tap into it and see what awesome reserves you find there to make it happen!

Again, remember that the tremendous power of positive thinking, self-talk and empowering beliefs can seriously help us change the way we think and feel about ourselves over time. Like the well- known term, 'Self-Fulfilling Prophecy", if we truly come to believe and act on the concept, it can become part of who we are, and ultimately, want to be.

With these songs now available on your personal playlist for ***determination/persistence***, they will be ready when you need and implement this significant life skill message. Your confidence and ability to deal more effectively with determination and persistence is strengthened as a result! Use it regularly going forward!

Mindfulness & the Music/Questions to Ask Yourself & Self-Reflect -

After listening to the songs, take some time and give these questions some serious thought. Your answers here will reveal a great deal to you going forward. Use this opportunity for helpful self-reflection.

<u>Do you ever experience periods of self-doubt? How frequently?</u>

<u>Describe how you approach self-doubt and how you deal with it personally?</u>

Do you struggle with fear? If so, fear of?

Do you allow your fears to immobilize you at times? What can you do to embrace them head-on?

Currently, how would you describe your self-esteem? Do you need a change there?

What gets in the way of a healthy self-esteem for you? What can you do to personally make it better for yourself?

Are you thankful and optimistic for your own victories, however small they may be? Why do they make a difference with remaining positive?

The Reflective Journaling Process -

Now, take a deep breath, relax, and take the time to really think about your responses to the above mindful questions. What are your reactions, thoughts, and feelings regarding these meaningful questions? Is it difficult for you to provide concrete answers? I encourage you to write down your responses in the space allocated here to save and have access to later. This is your special time set aside just for you. The focus, personal awareness, and self-discovery that results from this therapeutic process will reveal a great deal to you regarding this essential life skill and how it impacts you personally. Your answers will empower you and provide you important feedback about addressing this life skill the very best you can.

Journaling Notes

_____

_____

_____

_____

_____

_____

_____

_____

_____

_____

_____

_____

Recommended Reading about Music & Song -

- "Music Builds Self-Confidence" by Samantha Manus, savethemusic.org, November 24, 2016

Chapter 17

Life Skill Theme – *Positivity*

The Song Playlist -

1. "Unwritten" by Natasha Bedingfield

2. "Lovely Day" by Bill Withers

3. "Daisies" by Katy Perry

4. "Can't Stop the Feeling" by Justin Timberlake

5. "What a Wonderful World" by Louis Armstrong

6. "Me!" by Taylor Swift

7. "Beautiful Day" by U2

8. "I Gotta Feeling" by Black Eyed Peas

9. "Happy" by Pharrell Williams

10. "Don't Worry, Be Happy" by Bobby McFerrin

Emotional Needs Analysis

If you ever need a quick uplifting shot of positivity and self-esteem, this is definitely a playlist to listen to. These days, life can be daunting and at times it can be difficult to see any light at the end of the tunnel. We all really need those diversions into the light providing us that hope, faith, and purpose, those essentials that keep us going. This playlist is especially meaningful for those who may be just starting out on the life journey, or those seeking a new direction to embark on. The message is so empowering, you feel like you can tackle just about anything life throws your way after listening to it. It definitely inspires with a joyous refrain, "yes, you certainly can !!!"

How many of us are plagued by periods of self-doubt and second-guessing ourselves? The road to truly believing in our abilities and potential can be a tricky one indeed. Sometimes it simply comes down to the fact that we just don't know where to start, and it can become overwhelming. What we want within our heart, what others want for us, suggestions, advice, warnings, the list can go on and on. Sometimes we feel like we are pushed and pulled in a thousand different directions and we don't know which way to turn. Learning how to silence all the noisy distractions, trust, and listen to your inner voice and your ability to make sound decisions that you feel are specifically right for you. After all, who knows yourself better than you do!

I find this playlist is also a mantra of support to those we know and care about, for who may be unsure, undecided, and struggling. Those words of encouragement are always eagerly accepted, valued, and never forgotten. It can make such a significant difference to those who may need it to stay on track. And thus, we all want to give each other whatever we can to make the journey better. Have you ever asked yourself whether you are a positive risk-taker? Are you ready and willing to take a chance, make a needed change, or embark on a new, different path in life? We need to let go of the past that can limit us, including those mistakes that everyone makes. We need to reach out, try again, and embrace life in the process of becoming who we want to be. I see this playlist as one of inspiration, challenge, happiness, and enthusiasm. On a personal basis, my extraordinary and giving mother taught my siblings and I to always believe and strive for the best we can be. The way she lived her life and the amazing life lessons she provided to our family are part of who we are today. Even if you feel you may not be ready, it gets you in the habit of regular helpful reflection and provides you food for positive thought.

Your personal book of life lies open before you in many aspects. It's right before you as you create and fill in the empty pages with your unique story. What will you write for yourself? As you venture forward, give yourself an open opportunity to experience life fully, as best as you can. Believe in yourself. Be careful of "settling." Always give yourself that push to do better, aim for success, strive for more, as long as you don't overwhelm yourself in the process. Life is truly a gift, and our time on earth is limited. Let's make it a joyous, fulfilled one!

Takeaway Thought for the Week Ahead -

Takeaway positive thoughts empower you, give you strength, make you believe. Here is yours for the week. <u>Say it several times a day, every day. Memorize it, write it down, or put it in your phone. During the week, make it a daily routine; rely on it as you make it your own.</u>

Every day can bring change within us. So, all we can ask of ourselves in life is to try for the best we possibly can achieve. Always strive for positivity. Believe that it is yet to come.

Again, remember that the tremendous power of positive thinking, self-talk and empowering beliefs can seriously help us change the way we think and feel about ourselves over time. Like the well- known term, 'Self-Fulfilling Prophecy", if we truly come to believe and act on the concept, it can become part of who we are, and ultimately, want to be.

With these songs now available on your personal playlist for ***positivity***, they will be ready when you need and implement this significant life skill message. Your confidence and ability to deal more effectively with building positivity is strengthened as a result! Use it regularly going forward!

Mindfulness & the Music/Questions to Ask Yourself & Self-Reflect -

After listening to the song, take some time and give these questions some serious thought. Your answers here will reveal a great deal to you going forward. Use this opportunity for helpful self-reflection.

Do you believe you have a healthy self-esteem? If not, why? Has it changed recently?

Do you routinely doubt the decisions that you make? If so, when does that happen?

Since childhood, do you feel your family promoted a sense of positive self-esteem within you? If not, why not?

Do friends and other people in your world build up your sense of self-esteem rather than bring it down? If not, why do you think you give them that power over your own self-awareness?

What feelings do you personally struggle with in term of your self-esteem? Does that hold you back from becoming the person you truly want to be?

Do you regularly try to surround yourself with positive people who encourage and support you as they bring out the best within themselves and in particular you?

Do you routinely set aside time out of your daily schedule for self-reflection concerning your life and who you are and want to be?

What are some of the strengths you possess that you are of most proud of? What do those strengths say about you? Think about them and acknowledge them whenever possible. Most of all, believe what those strengths say about you. You will become the unique, special person you believe you are.

To increase your individual self-esteem and positivity, name three to five areas you feel you need to work on going forward. Why do you feel they are important to you?

The Reflective Journaling Process -

Now, take a deep breath, relax, and take the time to really think about your responses to the above mindful questions. What are your reactions, thoughts, and feelings regarding these meaningful questions? Is it difficult for you to provide concrete answers? I encourage you to write down your responses in the space allocated here to save and have access to later. This is your special time set aside just for you. The focus, personal awareness, and self-discovery that result from this therapeutic process will reveal a great deal to you regarding this essential life skill and how it impacts you personally. Your answers will empower you and provide you important feedback about addressing this life skill the very best you can.

Journaling Notes

_____

_____

_____

_____

_____

_____

_____

_____

_____

_____

_____

_____

Recommended Reading about Music & Song -

- "How Music Therapy is Reducing Anxiety and Isolation" by Wilson Chapman, discovermagazine.com, November 2nd, 2020

Chapter 18

Life Skill Theme – *Reaching Out*

The Song Playlist -

1. "You Found Me" by the Fray

2. "Reach Out and Touch" by Diana Ross

3. "One Call Away" by Charlie Puth

4. "You'll Be in My Heart" by Phil Collins

5. "I'll Stand by You" by the Pretenders

6. "Keep Holding On" by Avril Lavigne

7. "Umbrella" by Rihanna

8. "All You Wanted" by Michelle Branch

9. "Arms Open" by The Script

10. "Here I Am" by Leona Lewis

Emotional Needs Analysis -

As a therapist I am thrilled to be able to suggest these very powerful songs for your playlist dealing with reaching out and connection. In particular, I think this theme is an excellent one, essential to our emotionally healthy well-being. The music outstanding, the lyrics so profound, all with very meaningful messages, that we can certainly learn from. The lyrics ask us to dig pretty deep within ourselves. Exploring those reflections of our belief system, faith, essential values, and our personal journey dealing with life and relationships, inspiring us as listeners.

Reaching out and connecting with others has never been more important and needed than today. Even in the age of Covid restrictions, we need to maintain those important social interactions. Whether every day or holiday celebrations of rejoicing, gifting, and/or important end-of-the-year reflections, social interactions with family and friends are necessary to keep us in tune with each other. With the intense changes and restrictions forced by the reality of living with Covid and the variants out there, it is definitely different, requiring much forced adjustment on our part. It may not be as easy as it once was, or what we are used to. But, bottom line, the need for reaching out remains integral for our emotional and mental health well-being.

The truth is many people may struggle with isolation and disconnection from others. I see many sad and lonely people reaching out to me as a therapy provider. People dealing with personal disappointments, regrets, indecision, and loss. I always remind them, yes, you have taken that important first step. You are proactive and have reached out for help. You are asking for change for the better. That is really the foundation for moving forward positively. We, as psychotherapy providers, always see an increase in intake calls from people in need especially proceeding the start of a new year. It is indeed a vulnerable time for many and we need to be alert and responsive to this. Specifically, we need to be ready and available to reach out and connect with others who may be asking for our help-ing hand.

With these intense emotional lyrics that touch on the universal needs to be there, reach out, connect, and in particular, give love and care, the message is perfectly clear. Bottom line, isn't love and care the foundation of everything that life is about? Love is the core that makes us do all these great things for others. If anything, do it for love. I find this song playlist is a plea for all of us to be aware and present for those in need. They may not outwardly show or voice the struggle to us directly, but in many cases, it's there, waiting and hoping for someone, somewhere, to be a safety net. So many feelings are reflected throughout the lyrics here... those of inse-curity, bewilderment, loneliness, confusion, anger, and sadness. When you feel some days it's difficult to put one foot in front of the other. But some-how, you find the inherent will and determination to do it, with a sense of optimism, a hope eternal, for someone to embrace you with love and care. For others, they may still be out there struggling, continuing to wait for some sign, from someone. You can certainly be that someone.

In today's fast-paced world where so much is expected or demanded of us every day, life can sometimes be draining. The common thought, "so much to do, so little time, such limited energy", is indeed true. Yet, we have to try to make the time, to find the time, not only for ourselves, but for others around us who basically need us. Because they may be silent about their struggles, we must become aware and present as much as we possibly can. Why and what are we waiting for? What is the purpose in holding it back? What is stopping us from ultimately taking action? Consider making that long-awaited phone call, finally make that overdue visit, send a text message, send an invitation, email, letter, or card. Don't allow regrets to enter the picture later and complicate things. Let someone know you are thinking of them today and that you're there for them. Knowing they are loved and cared for may make such a significant difference in someone's world and personal outlook going forward. It may turn everything around for them, and in the process, be such a source of joy for you throughout the year. You would want it done for you, so consider it a wonderful form of paying it forward!

Takeaway Thought for the Week Ahead -

Takeaway positive thoughts empower you, give you strength, make you believe. Here is yours for the week. <u>Say it several times a day, every day.</u> <u>Memorize it, write it down, or put it in your phone. During the week, make</u> <u>it a daily routine; rely on it as you make it your own.</u>

As we reflect on these most challenging times and think about approaching the coming year with a positive, hopeful perspective, remember... it's never too late to reach out to someone in need. It's never too late to show someone you care. Give the time and effort required because you will never regret it. Wouldn't you want someone to do the same for you when you're struggling? Pay the love forward. Yes, do it for them, but also, do it for you.

Again, remember that the tremendous power of positive thinking, self-talk and empowering beliefs can seriously help us change the way we think and feel about ourselves over time. Like the well- known term, 'Self-Fulfilling Prophecy", if we truly come to believe and act on the concept, it can become part of who we are, and ultimately, want to be.

With these songs now available on your personal playlist for *reaching out*, they will be ready when you need to implement this significant life skill message. Your confidence and ability to deal more effectively with reaching out is strengthened as a result! Use it regularly going forward!

Mindfulness & the Music/Questions to Ask Yourself & Self-Reflect -

After listening to the songs, take some time and give these questions some serious thought. Your answers here will reveal a great deal to you going forward. Use this opportunity for helpful self-reflection.

If given the opportunity, do you generally reach out to people you know?

If not, why do you feel you don't? Being perfectly honest, are there factors that prevent you from doing so? If so, can you specify them?

Are you aware of people in your world who are struggling emotionally? Can you identify them and provide any reasons why?

Are you comfortable being around and encouraging those people? If not, why not?

Are there specific things you can actively do to help them feel better?

Do you feel you are an open, emotionally giving type of person?

Do you routinely take the time to check up or check in with friends?

Do you follow through with keeping in regular touch with your friends? In what way/s?

Do you feel that people reach out to you when you are in need? How do you generally respond to that? Do you find it personally helpful?

The Reflective Journaling Process

Now, take a deep breath, relax, and take the time to really think about your responses to the above mindful questions. What are your reactions, thoughts, and feelings regarding these meaningful questions? Is it difficult for you to provide concrete answers? I encourage you to write down your responses in the space allocated here to save and have access to later. This is your special time set aside just for you. The focus, personal awareness, and self-discovery that result from this therapeutic process will reveal a great deal to you regarding this essential life skill and how it impacts you personally. Your answers will empower you and provide you important feedback about addressing this life skill the very best you can.

Journaling Notes

_____

_____

_____

_____

_____

_____

_____

_____

_____

_____

_____

Recommended Reading about Music & Song

- "Harness the Power of Music to Heal Now" by Wayne Jonas, MD, psychologytoday.com December 17, 2019

Chapter 20

Power of Music & The Song

This book introduces you to the meaningful power of music, a song and its lyrics, that is in essence, therapeutic. As the name "Song Therapeutics" implies, the simple act of active listening and processing a song can truly be transformative and impact you emotionally. In so many significant ways, it can affect your thoughts, your feelings, your mood and outlook, your positivity, your hope! In that particular song, whether it touches on your relationships, your self-concept, your daily struggles, your losses, your joy, overall your life journey, it just makes so much sense. In today's fast-moving, complicated world, a song can affect us like nothing else can. The music, the instrumentation, the words, and especially, the message behind those lyrics. Let the music and the message speak to you on a personal level and help you as you learn.

As a licensed professional mental health therapist in private practice, as well as a consummate music lover, to me, the process couldn't be clearer. When I utilize lyrical songs to assist many of my clients within their individual therapy sessions, it has proven to me to be a highly therapeutic tool. A highly effective way to reach them, making a substantial difference in my interpersonal connection with them, as we focus on issues they are struggling with. For those who may be confused, may not understand just what they might be feeling, or may be unable to put their thoughts and emotions specifically into words, a familiar song can be their voice and can give them the clarity they may be looking for. Listening to the words of a song brings out, helps to identify, and helps to understand emotions, and thus, put them into words. This is especially beneficial and needed when those feelings may become overwhelming, so intense or confusing to be able to self-identify in spoken words. That is where the lyrics of a song can really work it's remarkable magic. Suddenly when you hear a certain song, those feelings and thoughts can become so apparent, so identifiable, and suddenly, you're able to describe or put your thoughts and feelings into words. Simply put, the lyrics may assist you in getting it right. The lyrical messages can help express, clarify, and uplift what's in your mind and heart. Whether we realize it or not, we are continuously learning from the lyrics we hear in song. They impact us significantly with their messages. The messages affect either us positively or negatively, so let's learn from them and take these lessons a step further.

We should always try to gain something positive and proactive with what we hear. I think of it visually like a square box, four equal sides, four aspects, with the contents enclosed inside. I like to call it my four A's to becoming proactive. Specifically, this consists of awareness, acknowledgement, action, and, finally, adaptation. These four aspects or lessons result in the resulting learning experience.

Besides the pure enjoyment and aesthetic value of music, these are essentially the four powers at work when you actively listen to song lyrics. Simply put, if a song becomes personally meaningful for you, you begin the process of identification. On an individual level, your personal *awareness* increases, you may *acknowledge* similarities or differences with your life experience, you may possibly take *action* to change something, and ultimately, you *adapt* accordingly to what you learn and works for you. This is always undertaken with the hope, and eventual goal, of enhancing positivity and being proactive in your life, whenever you can.

Chapter 21

Heart & Soul of the Lyrics

The essence of this book concept emerges from the heart and soul of the lyrics, created by the amazing musician/singer/songwriter. A song and its lyrics can essentially tell a story of some kind and provides an over-all message to the listeners. These extraordinary musicians make up the musical fabric of our life. The list of names we may be familiar with is basically endless, and their creative efforts should always be recognized and applauded.

Without any doubt, one familiar name at the top of the list is Bruce Springsteen. A skilled musician, singer, and brilliant songwriter, his impressive musical portfolio, his words and music, shows us simply that he just gets it. With Springsteen's music, I often think to myself in terms of his lyrical mindset, *where does all this impressive understanding come from?* The psychological connection, the relating, the identification with common human emotions, the pure transparency. I felt that it was always real for him and coming from pure truth within his heart and soul. Years ago as I was reading his wonderful and candid autobiography, *Born to Run*, it became very clear to me. Springsteen was living and breathing life experiences every day, along with a myriad of deep thoughts and feelings, so he was bound to put it so brilliantly into the body of his music. His songs would undoubtedly reflect the emotions within and what he was experiencing in his personal life. His family history, his hardships, his romantic connections, his daily life, as well as emotional and mental health struggles that he so openly and beautifully describes for the benefit of others. Springsteen did a fantastic album recently, entitled *Letter to You*. The title track reflects directly how his writing throughout the years reflected his emotional and psychological journey. To me, with the purpose behind Song Therapeutics and this book, I see that song as an extremely important explanation. I see the letter as Springsteen's body of music. His words are his music. His song lyrics are so real and provide us universally with such great messages dealing with a wide range of common feelings such as joy, pain, fear, doubt, and struggle. The process of his looking inward through his music with openness and truth that we can all be inspired by, in addition to encouraging our own mindfulness for the future.

Another significant musical artist on the list that I feel must be mentioned here is the late, great Tom Petty. Whether as a solo artist or with his longtime band, The Heartbreakers, Petty also possessed the gift of weaving heartful, meaningful lyrics into those wonderful musical backgrounds. His songs frequently touched on many examples of our common human emotions and experience. Scenes and situations complete with musical dialogue, taken from daily life as he was known to do so well, for so many years. His sudden, tragic death a few years ago truly left a huge void within the worldwide musical community. But luckily, we will always have his amazing music to listen to, reflect, share, and enjoy forever, as will future generations benefiting from his outstanding musical catalog.

Musicians/singers/songwriters have the courage, honesty, energy, and the willingness to go there to help others through their music. What a gift to give, again, a legacy that will always go on. A musical gift that reaches and touches most people in some form every day, making a difference in so many lives. I cannot even imagine a world without music, and if so, how empty that would be, in so many essential ways. We are thankful for those who share not only their talent and music offerings with us but their emotional journey as well. What are those songs, those playlists that are meaningful to you, that make a personal impact and touch your heart and soul? Have you already identified them and are using them? I hope this book and the songs and playlists that I have suggested will help you understand and find your way, whatever issue you may encounter in life.

A creative, professional musician with an accomplished portfolio, Jeff Miers is the resident music critic for the *Buffalo News* since 2002. His extensive music reviews and critiques are well known and highly respected within the Western New York music community and beyond. Jeff Miers' acute interest and knowledge in the realm of music is reflected in his receiving the distinguished President's Award from the Buffalo Music Hall of Fame in 2014. He concurs that "people are actively listening and truly reconnecting with music and lyrics again, like they never have before." When I asked Jeff if he could provide some affirmative thoughts regarding music today, he wrote something I am pleased to be able to share here: "Throughout my life, I have turned to music for solace and comfort during the darkest times, and for inspiration and education even during the best of times. It is by now a bit of a cliche to suggest that music heals, but in my own life, I've been given every indication that this is exactly the truth. Music, the act of making it, yes, but also the act of listening to it, closely, can, over time, teach us empathy, allow us to forgive ourselves, urge us to strive for excellence, greatly bolster our imaginative capacities, and remind us repeatedly, that we are not alone as we navigate the complexities of our time on this planet. Music is a language that connects us, at the deepest, most primal and profound level, to our fellow human beings. But even in solitude, actively listening to and engaging with music can lead us away from the darkness and towards the light." A most profound, beautiful summary from him regarding the immense power of music in our lives today that I am thankful and honored to quote.

Chapter 22

Music & the Brain

Brain-based research backs up the process showing there is a definite scientific linkage between music and the brain as it relates to active listening! The scientific data is in, and the outcomes cannot be disputed. Knowledge is undoubtedly power, and it actually all lies within you. When people make comments such as "music simply makes my thinking better," "music just clears my mind," or "when I listen to that song, it touches my heart and mind," there is an undeniable reason and truth behind those words. Today's brain-based research definitely backs up the fact that the act of active listening and connecting to music enhances the level of one's left-brain activity and the limbic system, which controls emotions. The limbic brain regions (amygdala) are strongly affected by music and song. It definitely confirms a strong brain-based linkage between the two, enhancing one's emotional/mental health as well as physical well-being.

Exciting new findings in the realm of brain-based psychology have emerged regarding the meaningful link of therapy used with music and song. Professor Jorg Fachner and Dr. Clemons Maidhof of Anglia Ruskin University recently published their important findings: (*"Brains Work In Sync During Music Therapy: Researchers Make Major Breakthrough Using Brain Hyperscanning"*, *www.sciencedaily.com/ July 25, 2019*), and as a therapist, I found this study in particular quite fascinating. For the first time, researchers have been able to demonstrate that the brains of a patient and therapist became synchronized during a music therapy session and was the first music therapy study to use hyperscanning, a procedure which records activities of two brains at the same time, allowing them to better understand clinically how people interact with each other. In that way, the researchers were hoping for a breakthrough that could basically improve future interactions between patients and their therapists in session. During that specific research session, classical music was played as a client discussed a serious illness that was currently going on in her family. Both the therapist and the client wore electroencephalogram (EEG) caps that contained sensors that captured electrical signals in their brains. This interaction was recorded in sync using video cameras with the EEG. During the study, it was noted at one point that the client's brain activity shifted suddenly from displaying deep negative feelings to a more positive feeling shift. Soon afterwards, as the therapist saw that the session was positively working by client verbal affirmation, their scan displayed similar results to the client's. When interviewed later, both the client and therapist stated that particular moment in session as the pivotal point when they felt the therapy was positively working in sync, and making a difference. Therapists all look for those moments where we feel we are making that significant connection with our clients. It can be classified as life-altering moments of change. The activity in the brain's right and left frontal lobes where negative and positive emotions are processed, respectively, were thoroughly examined. Through thorough analysis of the hyperscanning data alongside the video footage, as well as a transcript of the verbiage from that particular session, the researchers were able to demonstrate that brain synchronization definitely occurs, and physically just what a therapist–client moment of change looks like inside the brain. What a fantastic milestone and breakthrough in the utilization of music and song in therapy with clients!

It clearly demonstrates that emotional connections and changes are indeed experienced during those therapeutic interactions. The findings of their study definitely confirmed this theory using definitive brain data. Without a doubt, music and song used in psychotherapy can improve engagement, well-being, positive feelings, and self-esteem. It can be effectively used working with those clients struggling with anxiety, depression, and a host of other emotional/mental health issues, as well as individuals with autism and dementia. Besides clients verbally confirming their positive changes to us during the therapy session, the research and data from this dynamic hyperscanning study confirm it with hard factual data. We can clearly see what's happening in the brain, and the results are very exciting, confirming such positive outcomes with our clients. This also opens up the door to future research, clinical findings, and practice application in this realm.

Subsequently, the quality of your emotional functioning is affected regardless of your musical tastes or preferences. In other words, music sharpens your brain and healthy emotional functioning level, and subsequently you are more in tune with your inner thoughts and feelings. An active, engaged brain remains a much healthier brain for a longer period of time. Active listening is the act of focusing, really paying attention, and fully concentrating on the message being conveyed in the lyrics, rather than just passively "hearing" the music. Your brain is thoroughly in full cycle during this process. It is thinking, comparing, evaluating, assessing what is heard, and, whether helpful if we compare with our own personal situations. The term "identification" explains it very concisely. Depending on your personal situation, you can identify and relate to thoughts and feelings a song may convey. Oftentimes, a song puts everything in perspective for you and makes a notable difference.

Chapter 23

Identifying Mood Music

Take advantage of the many positive mental health benefits that can result from meaningful song experiences. Continue to build up your personal playlist with great selections, so really take the time to listen and reflect on the message being said. Try to include listening to those songs you need as a regular, important part of your day. Besides what song lyrics convey to us, we all respond to the music we hear in very individualized ways. When we hear familiar songs, they may remind us of certain emotional responses or situations we experienced when hearing them before. Simply described as an "imprint" on the brain, they can quickly bring us back to those familiar feelings or mood. What we label "Mood Music" does not have to be lyrical to reach you emotionally or psychologically; instrumental music can touch your soul.! Our mood definitely influences the music selections we make. The sound, the beat, the instrumentation can effectively bring you there emotionally as well. What are we looking for, and specifically what do we feel we need at the time? In seeking out music for relaxation, will it be deep, soothing, and calming; music to help us focus during work or study; or uplifting or re-energizing to provide us that needed boost. We seek out those sources of relaxation through mood music which we select and works in a variety of ways.

And today, many people are returning more frequently to the safety and reliability of radio programs to meet their music, information, conversation, and relaxation/stress management needs.

As you seek out forms of mood music to achieve or enhance your sense of calmness or relaxation, certainly be aware of the volume and tempo. Loud sounds may be physiologically stressful with a tempo that can be faster than your resting heartbeat. That can in turn increase your blood pressure, breathing, and heart rate. A slow tempo and rhythm slows everything down within your body and works to promote that deep relaxation. This is attained through long musical notes or at times even soft, subtle sounds taken from nature. To be able to focus more efficiently, listening to solo or limited instrument pieces may be indicated. A faster tempo with more complex instrumentation will tend to energize your mind and body. Musicians routinely compose and utilize their instruments to create and deliver an entertaining body of musical work to you as the listener. They often do this without lyrics, using only the music itself, to make that emotional and psychological connection with their audience. What are their goals, what is their intent, what is the creative process like for them?

Thomas Mariano, a talented young musician and a brilliant keyboardist from the Rochester, NY, area, composes, records, mixes, and masters his recordings. Mariano states, "My personal objective, first and foremost, is to make the listener feel and experience. As humans we are biologically predisposed to certain responses and certain sonic qualities. It is fairly easy to see how these reactions aided us during evolution. As musicians, we manipulate these reactions by carefully arranging sounds to generate subconscious responses leading to noticeable emotions. Active listening especially to more complex music stimulates brain activity, and keeping our brain healthy is paramount to positive mental health. Yes, when I write a song, I do one of two things, 1) I have a passage I like and I think about what I associate that passage with, 2) From that point, I build around that to more clearly communicate a message." Along with fellow skilled musicians, drummer Chris Palace and bassist Jordan Rabinowitz, their excellent CD/digital album, *Dream Float #2*, combines many elements of instruments and unique sounds to create an amazing musical experience for listeners, which definitely includes a beneficial psychological aspect.

In essence, what we hear ultimately affects what we think and feel deep inside, so take the time and opportunity for learning to use music and song as a lifelong tool to effectively navigate you through the daily ups and downs we all encounter along the way. So many incredible benefits await… improvement of mood, focus, attending skills, academic test scores, memory, as well as social connection. Music is ingrained in so many critical areas of our life!

Chapter 24

Benefits of Hopeful Music

People routinely ask me if music and lyrical song can actually provide the concept of hope and help them feel better about their lives. The simple answer is a resounding, YES!!! Think of it as an effective strategy that is basically quick, easy, and enjoyable to use. You love and routinely listen to music/song in your life, why not let its power of meaningful lyrics benefit you whenever or wherever you need it, for, whatever reason?

So…here are the 10 Positive Reasons to Listen to Hopeful Music, Every Day…

1. *Gives you a workable plan or strategy to get you what you want or where you want to go;*

2. *Provides you internal motivation to consider and encourage making needed change in your life;*

3. *Helps you with overall stress and anger management;*

4. *Builds creativity, mindfulness, and a proactive mindset;*

5. *Stimulates problem and decision-making skills through self-reflective thinking;*

6. *Decreases anxiety, improves mood, and basic outlook on life;*

7. *Strengthens personal resiliency and self-control abilities;*

8. *Boosts level of happiness, hope, and optimism about one's future;*

9. *Improves your mental/emotional and physical wellbeing as well as general health/immunity; and*

10. *Builds your overall self-esteem by empowering you to truly believe in yourself.*

Chapter 25

Personal Action Plan

When true learning occurs, some significant things result that greatly impact your self awareness, enlightenment, and especially, the possibility of implementing change or improvement. Begin this important process by putting your self-discovery and what you have learned into a targeted personal action plan that is correct and meaningful for you. Gaining this information and being proactive helps build your self-esteem and level of empowerment.

After you are done listening to all the songs on the playlists presented, you have done some important reflection and journaled your thoughts, now think of how the life skill themes of the various playlists affects your life specifically.

Expanding on all of this, think of a situation, circumstance, or particular person that comes to mind and *if you feel change or improvement in any specific life skill is warranted*, based on your individual needs. You are taking charge here, so believe and trust your self-knowledge. What will your personal action plan look like? What will it involve? Will it reflect needs that become essential when making your decisions for the plan to work?

Any effective action plan will call for setting goals and objectives required for the plan to be realistic for you.

- What is the overall goal you wish to accomplish?

- What are the specific steps, or objectives, that will help you get there?

Begin to think of your personal action plan as a road map of life. It will guide you along your path as you work to bring it to reality.

In formulating an effective personal action plan, here is a quick checklist of 8 important considerations necessary to remember beforehand:

- Consider your values and what is truly important to you.

- You will require healthy self-esteem to tackle positive change.

- Be aware that your emotional as well as physical energy will be needed for realistic change as well.

- Additional support from others around you is beneficial when considering implementing any kind of change.

- Set realistic goal/s needed for your action plan.

- Establish workable objectives or steps needed to achieve your goals and jump-start your action plan.

- Consider the advantages and disadvantages of decisions you are evaluating.

- Consider any risks involved with your decision-making options.

Bottom line, trust your instincts! You know yourself and the final choice is yours alone. It's always going to be up to you. I hope these song playlists, as well as the content and strategies presented in this book, help you formulate a pro-active personal action plan for what is right for you in the future!

Chapter 26

Your Personal Music Inventory

Your individualized musical preferences are important and say a whole lot about you, as your songs are a very powerful force. By reading this book you recognize and value the power of music and song in your life, and that you are wanting the lyrical messages to assist you on your journey. Becoming an aware, informed consumer of music, you will establish an excellent foundation for making those musical choices concerning what you specifically choose to listen to. This music inventory will provide self-assessment to help you do that. You will be more likely to seek out and utilize the songs, lyrics, and their messages if you are enjoying and specifically connecting with the music. Basically, this music inventory will assist you to further discover, clarify, and organize those musical preferences and favorite choices that are part of your life.

It is highly recommended that you take the time to review this 16 question Individualized Music Inventory after you complete reviewing all the playlists of songs featured within the book. See what your personal self-reflections will say about you. Music preferences often evolve and change over time; thus, it is always a good practice to regularly assess what you need and are looking for in your music choices. Take note of the changes you may have and what those changes reveal/signify about your current needs. Value your music and your song choices with those meaningful lyrics that have messages that will help you!

1. *Besides the lyrical message, did you personally connect with any specific song? The style, genre, instrumentation, artist? If yes, which song? Why? If no, why is that?*

2. *When seeking out music to listen to, what are you generally looking for? Would you classify it as... Rock; Pop; Country; Oldies; Heavy Metal; Classical/Opera; Indie; Rap/Hip Hop; Jazz; Rhythm/Blues; Easy Listening; Reggae; Folk; Electronic/Dance?*

3. *Do you have an overall favorite type of music? Why do you think that is?*

4. *What is your least favorite type of music? Why do you think that is?*

5. *Do you have a favorite musical group?*

6. *Do you have a favorite female singer?*

7. *Do you have a favorite male singer?*

8. *Do you prefer lyrical song choices or instrumental music choices?*

9. *Do you generally prefer solo musical artists or musical groups to listen to?*

10. *Do you have any music that tends to relax you?*

11. *Do you ever use music to help you fall asleep?*

12. *Does music affect your moods? In what way?*

13. *Do you have a favorite musical instrument? Have you ever played one?*

14. *Do you enjoy listening to "live" music performances and/or concerts? If so, what kind of music or what specific artists?*

15. *Do you use an audio streaming service to listen to music? If so, which one?*

16. *Do you currently compile playlists on your audio devices? If so, describe them.*

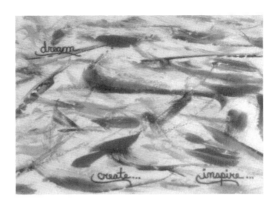

Chapter 27

Your Own Perfect Song

This is such a meaningful yet fun, creative activity for the mind, heart and soul. It's a great exercise to promote mindfulness, self-discovery and self-awareness. Many of us have a special, favorite song that we regularly go to and seek out for comfort and enjoyment. Many of the talented song writers we are familiar with, have created their own perfect songs that they are sharing with us.

But, what if we were to take on the exciting challenge of composing our own perfect song, a direct reflection of who we are? What would we want our song to be about? What would it sound like? Most important, what would the lyrics say about you and your life?

You would personally be the song's musical composer as well as it's lyricist. The words you choose for your own perfect song will undoubtedly say so much about who you really are, as well as what you find important in your life. The song will tell others something about you that you want them to remember. Give it some serious thought but also, have fun with it!

Let me help you start the process as you begin thinking about what you would like to include in your own perfect song...

- Your own perfect song would be in what musical genre?

- What would the general tempo of your song be?

- What musical instruments would provide the background for your song?

- Would you want to sing the vocal for your song?

- If not, who would you want to sing it?

- What would the mood and feelings of your song convey?

- What would be the primary message of your song?

- How would you describe or summarize what you would include in your perfect song?

Take the time to reflect upon and answer the preceding questions about your own perfect song. Brainstorm some thoughts and ideas about what you would want included. Write them down, think about them, expand and be creative with them. And especially, value them and make them your very own. Be sure to date it and keep the resulting lyrics handy and close to you. After all, your own perfect song awaits you when you are ready!!!!

Chapter 28

ABCs of Best Listening Practices

To make this the best possible listening experience, it may be helpful to include the following A to Z listening practices to your routine… Know your ABCs !!

A – Attention Is Everything!

B – Be Able to Fully Focus.

C – Close Your Eyes.

D – Dim the Lights.

E – Enjoy a Yummy Snack.

F – Free up Your Busy Schedule.

G – Get a Comfy Seat.

H – Heighten Your Awareness.

I – Ignore Distracting Thoughts.

J – Just Be Present.

K – Know When It's the Right Time.

L –. Light a Scented Candle.

M – Mindfulness Matters.

N – No to Needless Worry.

O – Observe Your Stillness.

P – Put on Your Earphones/Earbuds & Walk/Run.

Q – Quiet Noisy Thoughts.

R – Remember the Lyrics.

S – Silent Your Phone.

T – Turn off Your TV.

U – Understand the Messages.

V – Volume Adjustment.

W – Wind Down & Relax.

X – X Marks the Spot for Your Favorite Coffee, Tea or Cocktail.

Y – Yield All Your Anxiety.

Z – Zest for Some Meaningful Music.

Chapter 29

What People Are Saying about the Book!

- *"I'm really starting to listen closely to my music now, the words do actually tell me a lot of stuff about myself."—Tom K., Buffalo, NY*

- *"I always look forward to the playlists presented & Nancy's analysis, it has me really thinking about what I need to do to make things better in my life."—Kim W., West Seneca, NY*

- *"These playlists are really amazing! They are there for me, when I need them and I always feel better when I use them!"—Shaneka J., Erie, PA*

- *"The choice of song selections are great & the takeaway thoughts are so helpful! I keep saying them over and over to myself & I'm believing!"—Susan C., Hamburg, NY*

- *"I love the mindful questions that Nancy puts on there. It forces me to take time for myself and think, answering those questions gives me hope for what I have to do to be better."—Dave S., Lancaster, NY*

- *"Journaling my thoughts and feelings afterward is so helpful because it gets me thinking about what I need to do in the future, and Nancy's insight is the best!"—Nguyen T., Toronto, CA*

- *"I love the different life skill categories for the songs, we've all been there, the thoughts and information she presents push you to take responsibility & be positive!"—Cathy Z., Springville, NY*

- *"I appreciate the reading recommendations about music, I'm learning a lot of interesting things I never knew before!"—Dale M., Jamestown, NY*

- *"I like the action plan for life skills! I never used to think about these things before and how important this stuff really is."—Hector E., Dunkirk, NY*

- *"I just love the music inventory, I'm understanding and appreciating the music I choose to listen to and why!"—Tyra W., Lackawanna, NY*

- *"I appreciate the playlists of songs that's there available when I feel I need it. I think now I'll be understanding myself more clearer by listening to these songs."—Sandra N., Niagara Falls, NY*

- *"The song suggestions on the playlists are great, lots of different artists with different types of music, a nice variety!"—Andre B., Amherst, NY*

Chapter 30

Famous Folks With Some Thoughts About Music

"I accept chaos, I'm not sure whether it accepts me,"
by **Bob Dylan**

"Music touches us emotionally, where words alone can't,"
by **Johnny Depp**

"One good thing about music, when it hits you, you feel no pain,"
by **Bob Marley**

"I ignore all hatred and criticism, live for what
you create, and die protecting it,"
by **Lady Gaga**

"Music flames temperament,"
by **Jim Morrison**

"Music is spiritual. Good music business is not,"
by **Van Morrison**

"Music is a world within itself, with the language we all understand,"
by **Stevie Wonder**

"You can neither win or lose if you don't run the race,"
by **David Bowie**

"Rock music is not meant to be perfect,"
by *Ozzy Osbourne*

"Music doesn't lie. If there is something to be changed in this world, then it can only happen through music,"
by *Jimi Hendrix*

"I think music in itself is healing. It's an explosive expression of humanity,"
by *Billy Joel*

"I'll play it first and tell you what it is later,"
by *Miles Davis*

"The bottom line is that musicians love to make music and always will,"
by *Jennifer Lopez*

"There are only a few notes. Just variations on a theme,"
by *John Lennon*

"Music can change the world because it can change people,"
by *Bono*

"If you write great songs with meaning and emotion, they will last forever because songs are the key to everything,"
by *Elton John*

Disclaimer

The book, <u>Song Therapeutics & Playlists to Empower your Life</u>, does <u>not</u> quote specific lyrics from songs. The book focuses on the meaning of song lyrics in varied playlists. These interpretations reflect solely the author's, not necessarily the composer's, views. The book is intended to provide a source of general information for awareness, self-discovery, and educational purposes. Although this information is thought-provoking, enlightening, and provides self-awareness and comfort, it is not intended to provide, nor does it provide, specific advice or guidance to any one individual, nor is it intended to address, or addresses any one individual's specific circumstances or condition. The book is not intended to furnish any form of professional counseling therapy services of any nature and is not, nor is it intended to be, a substitute or replacement for individual psychological therapeutic intervention for the reader. No therapist–client relationship is intended to be formed or formed with anyone reading this book. Anyone sensing that they require their own individual counseling consultation or is looking to establish a counseling relationship with a therapist, social worker, psychologist, or psychiatrist for his or her specific needs should do so if they feel it is warranted. No readers should disregard the advice of his or her therapist, or delay seeking any form of professional counseling intervention, on the basis of any information or lyric interpretation presented in this book. Access to and use of the information and the lyric interpretations presented here are presented as is, with the intention to provide helpful, thought-provoking information, education, and self-awareness/ self-discovery to readers.